A Glimpse of Eden

With drawings
by Victor Ambrus

A Glimpse of Eden

Evelyn Ames

HOUGHTON MIFFLIN COMPANY BOSTON

1967

Books by Evelyn Ames

✻

Only the Loving
My Brother Bird
The Hawk from Heaven
(poems)
Daughter of the House
A Glimpse of Eden

FIRST PRINTING   R

For Amyas, who shared it with me,
and with gratitude to Bob

A Glimpse of Eden

I

WE THOUGHT WE KNEW what to expect. Several friends had been there and told us about it; some, even, had made the same trip we were to going to make, but we discovered that nothing, really, prepares you for life on the East African Highlands. It *is* life (I want to say), making our usual existences seem oddly unreal and other landscapes dead; that country in the sky is another world. No matter what is told about it, it retains an aura of the unknown, and curious misconceptions persist. "Won't it be terribly hot, in August?" we were asked many times, and: "You'll be out in the bush for a month, in tents? Why? When you've seen one elephant, you've seen them all!" We came to know what people would say, but even though we answered blithely and with what we took for knowledge, we were almost as much in the dark as they.

It is a world, and a life, from which one comes back changed. Long afterwards, gazelles still galloped through my dreams or stood gazing at me out of their soft and watchful eyes, and as I returned each daybreak, unbelieving, to my familiar room, I realized increasingly that this world would never again be the same for having visited that one. Nor does it leave you when you go away. Knowing its landscapes and sounds (even more, its silence), how it feels and smells — just knowing it is *there* — sets it forever, in its own special light, somewhere in the mind's sky. Painters of the Middle Ages used to separate their visions and glimpses of Edens from the mundane scenes of earth by a large and comfortable-looking lap of cloud. We are separated from this African Eden by Time: all history (and much prehistory, too) flows between. There is a word in Swahili meaning "the other side of the river" — *N-gambo:* pronounced as they do it, in three syllables, a struck gong of a word, full of reverberations that go on and on. For one vivid month, between one new moon and the next, we lived on the other side of the river.

Were I to try and find the beginning of what brought us to go on a tenting safari in order to see and photograph the animals, I should find it very difficult. One might say that it began with a letter from our friends Margaret and Nathaniel, telling us they had always dreamed of doing this, and would we consider joining them, but then one must go further back — to an impromptu call we made at their house perched on a great cliff overlooking the Pacific. "Wild Bird" is a unique house — the envy of its owner's friends and architectural colleagues — and that morning, which was the kind that makes you think of the first day of creation, every headland for fifty miles stood clear, and six hundred feet straight down a herd of sea lions bathed and barked in the waves' rise and fall. Our visit together out on a balcony overhanging that drop was rather like that of wild birds — knowing each other only slightly then, and we stopping off briefly on a hurried trip down the long rocky coast — yet very quickly we discerned that we moved on the same currents, and were nourished by the same things. And that takes one even further back, and forward, in Time: to Margaret as a little girl who loved to collect stones and still returned from travels with her luggage full of rocks; to my husband, Amyas, whose newest interest was collecting beach pebbles, polishing them and getting them set into jewelry, so that when Margaret saw the pebble bracelet on my wrist, the shock of a shared interest rang almost audibly in the air. In the more distant background I see myself as a girl — waiting for hours to find a bird by its song, or nursing young birds fallen from the nest, while my husband-to-be was growing up on a wild tract of woodland and lake in Massachusetts, raising pheasants and stocking ponds with trout. From childhood on, animals and wildlife had been important to us. To the Owingses they had become a cause. Ever since a great white sea lion had been shot, from the highway, by someone who could gain nothing more than to stop its moving, Margaret had waged a war of protection in which both she and Nat were now trying to preserve our national wild areas and the creatures that live in them.

But if the origins are too complex and interwoven to identify, the start of the journey (and that is all that "safari" means) was not: we crossed the river in Rome. It didn't matter that we had come from North Italy and — before that — New York, or that Margaret and Nat had flown in from Hawaii and that our setting out from Nairobi was still several days away; Rome was the point at which we ex-

changed one world for another. Some light from the adventure ahead of us already shone on those tawny façades and
resounded in the roar of the traffic; the Eternal City had
never seemed more an aggregation of man's accumulated
achievements all existing at once: automobiles streaming and
honking past posters of jets pasted onto Renaissance walls
over their classic foundations and Etruscan bones.

The last night before Africa we dined on the terrace of a
villa at the top of the Janiculum, guests of the architect who
was director of the American Academy. Looking at the
faces around the candlelit table — beautifully laid and itself
the height of civilized dining — I considered the company
and what it represented. There was a Roman noblewoman
of a family going back to the Middle Ages; an American
city planner and his wife who had returned that day from a
conference in Greece on how modern cities might best be
laid out; there were the four of us on the eve of departure —
as sequestered on that dark height of our own as on the
terrace where we sat; and there was a famous classicist, engaged in excavating under the lowest known level of the
Forum. He told us about it after dinner, sitting on the balus-
trade against the city's constellations; what they were dis-
engaging from the rubble of the Caesars' Rome was so much
older, he said, than anything else yet found that it went back
to wholly unknown religions and customs, inexplicable forms
of worship. We sat in a circle around him, troubled and
stirred by the new glimpses he was giving us back into Time;
here and there a cigarette glowed or light caught a lifted
glass, but until our host broke the spell no one asked a
question or spoke. Ancient and modern Greece and Rome;
civilizations older than either; Hawaii and the Pacific coast

and New York and New England; the first tracings of cities still fifty or a hundred years in the future — all this was held between us that evening, suspended — how? — in the invisible world of experience, memory, imagination. For our generation, this mystery is vastly deepened and widened by shrinking space and time; it seemed that night to quiver almost into visibility — a web of incomprehensible complexity, as though all civilizations combined into a kind of gigantic, eternal city.

This was what we were leaving behind. What we were going toward, across Time, was its direct opposite and that there is no right name for this opposite says a great deal about our language — even more about us and what has happened to us. For neither "eternal" nor "wilderness" will do. "Wilderness" is heavy with overtones of waste and desolation — just as "wild" sets up in the mind echoes of violence, lack of direction, even fury. (Is it because man has struggled so hard and so long to subdue what he is only part of, that he found it necessary to make it monstrous as well?) And there is something static about the word "eternal," whereas anything continuing timelessly, anything alive, is also necessarily changing and evolving. Time being the mystery it is, it is not surprising that words make a muddle of it — that we have no way of describing the past still alive in the present. Words, used in relation to such realities, can do no more than point in their direction; just as gazelles and wildebeest head like so many live weather vanes toward a lion, they indicate a presence — that is all. If what follows heads at all truly toward what was around us that month, and the effect it had on us, that is all I ask.

II

THE ITALIAN PENINSULA, seen from 35,000 feet, lay like a deeply wrinkled boot on the blue floor of the Mediterranean. Until one came to the heel: there a haze, probably of the sun lowering through the atmosphere, blurred every outline. The last thing to disappear was the island of Stromboli, floating in light as if in sky, its long plume of smoke streaming toward the darkening east. The sight of it was hypnotizing; face pressed against the cold little oblong of glass between us, I watched it melt away astern, flaunting that age-old panache. It seemed the last outpost of Europe and of the familiar, civilized world — a mountain, through which the interior of the earth poured seething flame.

Over the North African coast it was already dark — nothing to be seen anywhere but night. From time to time during the next four hours I looked out, shielding my eyes from our own lights, and only once saw what looked like a fire, warm and orange, with a sparkling spiderweb of whiter lights spread out nearby. An oil refinery in the Sudan, the

engineer told me when I visited the flight deck. He asked
where we were going and said he hoped to go on safari sometime himself; he had never done so. As he sat making minute
adjustments in the bank of instruments which were metering
and controlling the performance of our four jets, I thought
how they made possible what we were about to do. The high
plateaus of Kenya and Tanzania are surrounded by jungle
or desert; only the airplane makes them comparatively ac-
cessible. "We are terribly lucky," our guide was to tell us
over our first campfire: "fifty years ago we couldn't have
done this without great hardship and danger. Fifty years
from now it will be too late."

He came to our hotel to meet us the afternoon after we
had arrived in Nairobi, the strangeness of our surroundings
making it feel much later than it really was. All day the
expected and unexpected jangled together as if in a shaken
kaleidoscope — the softly overcast sky and cool air like England, but the morning full of strange bird calls and flutings
punctuated by a parrot's insistent "Ndeo! Ndeo! Ndeo!" —
the Swahili for "yes." African servants padded barefoot
across the courtyard, bearing breakfast trays, yet the many
children about were all so fair-skinned and towheaded we
might have been in Copenhagen. And the town — which
we explored on foot — is all contrasts and extremes: con-
temporary rectangular architecture next to Mohammedan
mosques; horribly ragged and crippled figures leaning
against shop windows glowing with imported cosmetics; the
pavements a stream of Indian women floating along in saris,
Sikhs in turbans, Pakistani girls wearing cuffed satin trousers
and tight tunics, their gauzy scarfs looped low on their
backs, proud and intelligent-looking young Africans with

self-assured manners and western clothes. You ask yourself
dizzily which continent you are on.

Long-anticipated meetings which are also weighted with
the future can feel very unreal; ours with our guide was
ridiculous as well. For a year and a half we had exchanged
letters and made plans, coming to know each other as well
as one can that way, and since morning we had been trying
to connect by telephone, but when we happened to pass the
Owings' door just as a man knocked and they opened it —
we all stood paralyzed and dumb. The stranger announced
himself (presumably saying "Bob Lowis, sir"), but with his
rapid and gentle English intonation it seemed to our ears to
run together into a foreign, even Russian-sounding name.
Who *was* this tall distinguished man with dark hair spring-
ing into waves, a prominent nose and sharply attentive look?
For what must have seemed to him interminable minutes
we all gazed at him challengingly. "It was like entering a
den of lions," he told us over drinks that evening, with an
intensely amused and amusing expression. For the next few
days, while he shepherded us around Nairobi — showed us
our first lions and gazelles in the National Park just outside
the city; took us for lunch with his parents at their coffee
plantation — we scrutinized one another like couples who
have become engaged by mail — we and Margaret and Nat
who were in a way taking each other on faith, and this
Scottish-born Kenyan who for the next month would be to
us a combination of teacher, protector, parent, guide. Perhaps our behavior on meeting was not so odd after all.

Three days later we set out — on a journey more crammed
with unknowns than any of us had ever faced before. Usually one is at least partially prepared for new places and not

the least of the traveler's delights is the feeling of recognition he has on seeing a sight of which he has some previous impression. A Greek temple on its cliff above the sea may exceed all expectations, at the same time giving you a sense of warm confirmation that yes, this is exactly the way you knew it must be, while even the more foreign scenes of the Orient, or the unfamiliar vegetation and beaches and reefs of the tropics, fit some image you may not even have been aware of until confronted with the reality itself. Nothing can really prepare you for Africa: it is too full of extremes and contrasts, too immense — a spectrum of creation so much wider and more vivid than anywhere else that it seems to require a new set of senses, or the rediscovery of lost ones. Also, if you live as close to the animals and nature as we did, the unconscious is stirred at levels deeper than anything "remembered": you are returned to times and experiences to which we have lost all other access.

Starting out, we felt like children again. The questions we asked! As the safari proceeded, they were to become less in number and more discriminating, but that first day they came as thick as the dust that boiled away behind us or encircled an oncoming car. What was the name of that tree? What did the secretary bird live on in such desert? Giraffes, here? Where there were still telephone poles and wires? "Candelabra euphorbia. Lizards and grasshoppers. They string them high enough so the giraffe can go under. . . ." Bob answered them all, feeding us information as it seemed appropriate and wanted, patiently telling the same thing over and over to minds filling too fast to be able to retain.

Not only was everything new but except on days when we moved camp nothing would be planned. Each day we

entered a void, going out roving the land without destination
in search of what we could find, returning when we felt like
it, and this can be oddly disquieting at first to twentieth-
century urban people used to living almost totally by means
of prearrangement and schedule. It was to take days and
days before my executive husband no longer asked Bob what
was planned for that day or (later) how did he "envisage
the morning's trip?" And for Nat, the architect — who must
imagine, design, commit to drawing boards and blueprints
everything that he does! — what a great moment when he
sat back in his camp chair, yielding to the unknown, and
said, beamingly, "Bob knows best!" Of our little group — so
infinitesimal out in that landscape and under that sky — Bob
did indeed know best, just as the world in which we would
slowly, clumsily and sometimes painfully find our place
knew so much more. But this we still had to experience and
learn, and I am getting ahead of my story.

A little crowd of the towheaded children staying at the
Norfolk Hotel gathered around us in the courtyard as the
two Land Rovers were packed and we prepared to leave.
Our khaki pants and jackets were shamelessly new —
pressed and clean as they would never be again. Margaret
and I experimented with tying dust-colored head-scarves
over our hair and I envied her, as I always would, her beautifully neat silvered dark hair, brushed straight back and
pinned into a roll on top of her head, her whole way of
wearing clothes and colors so that they belonged to her like
plumage to a bird. In another incarnation she could well
have been a Gallic queen, with that tall, stately carriage,
those calm good looks; they were the perfect outer aspect of
the artist who drew landscapes as controlled and sensitive

as those of Chinese scrolls, of the self-sufficient woman who treasured the solitude of her wild and lonely house.

Nat, whom I had first met standing before his own hearth, had made such a vivid first impression that even here — almost half the world and five years away — I still saw him against that memory; his whole appearance was warm and roundly solid — like the beautiful stones of the chimney breast behind him. A beaming smile made his cheeks more spherical, his brown eyes — always eager and full of feeling — became shinier and rounder still. They looked out now from under a hat he had brought from Hawaii — an oversize Stetson of coconut straw, circled with a wide band of two clashing shades of red. It was a hat that was to acquire a kind of life of its own — each day growing new curves and dimples, somehow reflecting in its lines its owner's moods. In the great seas of grass or against backgrounds of dry brush it stood out like a buoy — Nat's personal signal, the barometer of his feelings, a calendar of our days. We grew as fond of that hat as we did of its ebullient, irrepressible wearer.

Our group was fitted into two large Land Rovers — specially designed four-wheel-drive cars that don't need roads to travel on and have lots of window and storage space. We and Bob, our luggage and bedding went in the first one — the one with a big hatch which could be opened for viewing game and which had, along its dark green sides, the same long scratches from thorns and bush which scar the sides of rhinoceros and hippos. Up in front of the driver was a compass and an altimeter, and in a shelf along the top of the windshield, first-aid and snake-venom kits and fishing rods. Elsewhere were water bottles and biscuits, spare parts for the car, and a rifle — this for extreme emergency and only outside the National Parks, where firearms are not allowed. Except for the rifle, these things went everywhere we did in this vehicle which was our lifeboat, a ship's crow's-nest a fort. After every trip it was cleaned out and inspected; long before sunup each morning it was prepared for "roving" — supplies replenished, windows wiped and polished.

In the second car, loaded with tents, food, and all equipment needed for a month, rode the three African "boys": Ngugi, Kimani, Njorogi. Ngugi drove — "better than I do, in mud," Bob would reassure us in a rather uncomfortable situation some weeks later. He was the oldest of the three, with a dashing stance and smile; he always wore a bright crimson and purple tie, knotted, American cowboy fashion, around his bare throat. Kimani, when in Nairobi, was Bob's personal servant, and was the only one of the three who spoke a little English. Cooking on a grid over a wood fire, using a few blackened pots and an oven made of a petrol tin, he produced soups and main dishes and homemade bread that would put to shame many high-priced restaurants. When you went to the "kitchen" to say how fine a meal had been, he shuffled his feet and purred shyly, at the same time that he smilingly agreed with you, repeating gently, "*Ndeo, ndeo, M'sabu.*" Njorogi, smallest of the three, was a mysterious little figure with a furred round nut of a head and an unsmiling face that looked as if it had seen terrible things. He was a tremendous worker; everything was done very quietly, with a minimum of movement and fuss as he made beds and cleaned tents, washed and pressed clothes, set tables and waited on us at meals. We never figured out hundred feet through a thunderstorm and set them before us still steaming hot and not a drop spilled. After meals I saw how he washed the cutlery in hot suds, rinsed it and dried it and laid it away in a soft cloth inside a sectioned box.

It was eight o'clock on a cool, gray morning that this caravan headed west for the Mara-Masai Reserve, this time moving not only out of the familiar but right out of civilization. "A few days out here," Bob told us, "and you will have forgotten your other lives." We had a hundred and eighty miles to go. For a long time we drove between farms and plantations on surfaced roads lined with utility poles, but the wide green edges could have been nowhere else in the world. When you go along African roads you feel that all Africa must be on foot: there is a continuous patient procession of women carrying tremendous burdens, women with babies in slings on their backs, old men with a goat or a cow on a string, young people — some on bicycles — children, cattle. In Kikuyu country, the grass is scored with tracks printed into the deep red earth by cows as well as people: the roadsides are their pastures. Every once in so often you pass what looks like a festive outdoor celebration (and that morning the parties were held in a drizzle): twenty or more men, women and children sitting or standing about around a fire, someone cooking, and piles of fruit or tomatoes and eggs laid out nearby. It is a bus stop — the social gathering-place for miles around.

Little by little, large fenced ranches replaced farms and there were almost no pedestrians. When fences and finally electricity stopped, too, we found ourselves on the open uplands beyond the Great Rift Valley, the road running be-

tween what looked like enormous fields of ripe wheat. The
sun had come out and clouds laid violet shadows on distances which seemed even vaster than in our own West; the
sweeps of valley were so wide, the mountain rims so far
away and faintly blue you felt as if you were a little above
the earth, seeing the curve of its surface from the air. Here
and there we began to see giraffe floating weightlessly along,
little herds of Thomson's gazelle flicking their tails, zebra
grazing, but this is not the place to speak of them any more
than it was the time — for us — to stop and watch them;
we had too far to go before dark. Bob, knowing this better
than we, was strict about stopping, although his charges
found that a sure way to make him pull up was to offer him
a cigarette. There was another. Coming over a rise, we saw
his eyes narrow, felt his attention sharpen: a long line of
something, rather like very small boats, was furrowing the
grass, leaving a narrow dark wake in the tawny sea. . . . "Masai! Moving their village!" he exclaimed. From a little
nearer, engine turned off, we watched a procession of human
figures and donkeys — the little beasts swimming along in
grass up to their middles, carrying shields and cowhides and
big brown gourds. Sun glinted off ornaments on the figures
beside them and flashed from the tips of spears; the figures
themselves were the color of African earth. Although Masai
do build villages, they live for, by and with their cattle; when
new pasturage demands it, they take their few belongings
and build another village elsewhere. We were to see a lot
of these extraordinary people.

A few miles farther we passed a group of their tall, slender
warriors who, seeing us slow down, ran to greet us. Everything about them — skin, hair, the wood of their spears and

staffs, the single toga-like garment knotted over one shoulder, which the wind blew off their naked bodies — all was the same deep coppery red. Loops and circlets of beads dangled from the top rims of their ears; little bells of copper swung from the lobes; ornaments were woven into the massed narrow braids of hair they had dyed with red ochre and greased with fat. Before one could properly take in the curious splendor of their appearance and carriage, their extended hands were in the window and they were solemnly saying *Jambo, jambo*! The grip of their hands was firm and pleasing, their smiles broad. Masai live exclusively on milk and cow's blood — only the young men going off at times by themselves in secret to eat meat — and this gives them magnificent teeth, the glossiest skins and a smell very much like that of a milk-fed baby, mixed with wood smoke and cowhide. One cannot be near them without smelling it; their beads and weapons exude it. While Bob talked with them in part Swahili, part Masai, the young men stood beside the car, each with his weight on one foot and the other either drawn up like a crane's in a marsh or else straight out in front — like figures out of ancient Egypt. Occasionally they studied us and our clothes as we were studying theirs. If one caught their eyes, they quickly and gaily smiled back as if sharing the joke of our mutual strangeness.

Bob turned to us: they were inviting us to come to their village. The first time you are confronted with people living as they did thousands of years ago, so many things claim attention that only a few details remain. And so I remember of that first village chiefly a circle of low dung-covered dwellings — like huge ground-wasps' nests — around a dung-filled kraal (or corral); the smell and smoke of wood fires; the women's small shaved heads like polished black balls. And two distressing things: the flies clinging to faces and eyes which they didn't bother to brush off; and our utter inability to communicate so that when they addressed us gently but urgently I felt helpless, ungracious and gauche.

"What can we *do*, Bob, when we visit them?" We were back in the Land Rover, hurrying along to make up time.

"Just what you'd do when visiting anyone's house — show them you like it and them; don't hurry anything; smile at the children."

What about the children, we pressed him, could we give them anything? They liked candy, and gum, he said; we would stop and buy some at the next (and last) settlement. And snuff, he added. Nat never approved of the candy — spoil *those* teeth? But with the string of snuff he purchased he made great conquests.

Narok is a trading post with a few steel-roofed huts, a store run by an Indian shopkeeper, a bulletin board for regional announcements since it is the headquarters of the district. The Masai come here for the few articles they purchase: the beads and wire and cowrie shells for their ornaments; the cotton cloth they dye with red ochre and make into tunics and capes; swords and, when they can afford it, snuff. A group of them sat on the grass outside the store, wearing slung from their shoulders *kibuyu*, or milk gourds, glossy as chestnuts, outlined with rows of white cowries and colored beads. This was the last settlement we were to see for three weeks; being near the entrance to the Reserve, it is also a kind of frontier.

Just inside the gate, on the bank of a stream ("all set about with fever-trees" but not at all "grey-green" or "greasy"), we sat in the grass among flaming aloes, and ate cold roast chicken, fruit and cheese.

"Stay away from a bushy place like that!" Bob called out as I left the group. "A rhino could be hiding in there!" We had a lot to learn.

Far back the road had changed from macadam to dirt; now it dwindled to a double track and where the high plains shrank into what looked like rough orchards, it ran along the foot of the Mara Escarpment — a steep ridge over a thousand feet high, rugged and forbidding for all its sapphire afternoon haze. As with other such escarpments, the world appears to stop at its dividing wall, but when one looks in the other direction, toward Tanganyika, the golden plains — swelling into gentle ridges or breaking abruptly into a worn-down tooth of mountain — seem to run on forever. Here and there, grass fires set by the Masai to bring up new forage were trailing milky rainbow clouds, and patches of burn blackened the land. At one point we were obliged to drive straight through a fire — there was no way around it — grass crackling on either side of the track, smoke closing us into a yellow-bright, smothering canopy.

"Can we see from here where we are going to camp?" one of us asked when we emerged. No one had spoken for a long time.

"See that long ridge down there? Just about where that drops off at the end." It looked like the tip of an island, the ocean beyond.

"How far would that be, about?"

"Twenty miles, probably."

He drew to a stop, put his binoculars to his eyes and silently studied what was out there. In time, I came to think his eyes were to him what binoculars are to the rest of us, for they caught the slightest movement or unusual color, a mere dot of a bird. After prolonged and careful scrutiny, their clear, light blue — set very deep in his head — had the look of distance in them which you see in the eyes of sailors and pilots, but sharpened with something else at once wary and contemplative.

"Is the other car behind us?" he wanted to know, not taking the glasses down. We told him it was.

"What if the fires are near where we camp?" Fatigue, uncertainty, misgiving were as heavy among us as the smoke turning deeper and warmer-colored with the now slanting sun.

"We'll go somewhere else."

We left the road and cut across country. At the bottom of all that grass, the ground is harder and smoother than you would expect, but one has to stay clear of rocks and rock-hard termite mounds, concealed ditches and hollows of trampled and caked mud in which animals wallow. Unexpectedly, in the grass, two parallel shadows appeared and Bob scowled.

"If they're my tracks from five weeks ago that's fine. If they're not — we'll have to go somewhere else."

At our speed of around five miles an hour, the end of the ridge seemed to grow no bigger and often went off on one side or the other as we tacked like a sailing vessel to get around a line of trees or avoid a "burn." Would there be time to find another campsite if the first wouldn't do? And the fires — if they cut us off? Our questions, spoken and unspoken, were no longer about what was at hand.

"Bob — if I have to go out of my tent in the middle of the night?"

"You flash your light about carefully. If you see eyes, wait."

"Will the animal go away?"

"Probably."

Margaret wanted to know if a campfire didn't keep them at a distance.

"Not in Masai country — they're used to fires. Just look!"

"About lions . . ." I asked, remembering Joy Adamson writing of their roaring around camp and other people's stories of lions playing with tent ropes, "do *they* come into camp?"

"Sometimes."

"What do you do then?"

Bob's laugh was as merry as his answer was surprising: "Put my head under the pillow till they've left."

At first, his cautious *probably's, maybe's, occasionally's* concerning animal behavior left one like a child in the dark, frustrated and on the edge of anger. Why didn't he turn on the light and put an end to one's fear? Slowly I came to understand that refusal to reassure — to say (as it were) "See, it's only the curtain and not a lion at all": he had sheer respect for the unknown; he wanted us to have it, too.

Creaking like a ship at sea, we rocked along, the grass sweeping under us with a rustling sound, leaving in the air a strange scorched smell. That grass *was* our sea . . . like the wild oats on California hills but deeper, waving in the wind, brushed with delicate strokes of buff and rose and yellow-green yet predominantly lion-blond. Miles and miles of it, broken only by termite mounds and by the acacia trees which the giraffes browse, the silvery-spiked whistling thorn, hung with black baubles — each one a whole ant colony (each tree housing one queen), sometimes by blasted, dead trees which had been destroyed by elephants. On a mound of this grass, as we stopped again to let Bob look around, five heads raised up — there were ten round ears all in a row, and two heads, we saw, were framed in shaggy ruffs. When we drew closer, the two maned ones vanished and the three others dropped again until they became invisible. (*"Thirty* lions could be hiding here beside us and we wouldn't see them," Bob whispered.) Slowly they raised up once more and one beautiful lioness mounted a higher place where she became a statue of attention — never looking at us directly, scorning us with a magnificent disdain as she sniffed the wind, every muscle taut.

We gave her a wide berth and drove on, but our inner landscape had now changed from flat, black fatigue and misgiving to highest excitement and anticipation. Everyone had things to say again, we no longer looked for the end of the ridge and suddenly it was there and we had come to our campsite on the bank of the Mara and the tracks had been Bob's after all.

We walked into a grove of trees and looked at the river: opaque and brown, it swept around us in a wide curve with the grandeur of larger streams, dimpling and gurgling here and there as it flowed past the ten-foot-high banks and under tall palms and wild fig trees. On the opposite bank, and at a point thirty yards from us on our own side, were places where animals crossed over; the mud was crowded with footprints and enormous droppings. Behind us, the Escarpment had turned to violet. Chairs were brought out and tents put up, and then the day declined almost as suddenly as if someone with a lamp had walked out of a room and closed the door. We sat having drinks, quietly content, listening to the voices of the "boys" around the kitchen fire and the strange, excited barking of zebra. Our own campfire, at the edge of the little bluff, was slow in getting started; Bob got up and pushed a log toward the center when, just below him, came a roaring *hnoof, hnoof!* and the long-drawn-out swoosh as of a good-sized boat. We could just make out the heave of water and waves washing the river banks, then a hippo's mounded eyebrows and eyes — bright red in the beam of a

flashlight — and the huge shape behind. With another stifled grunt he submerged and moved upstream, away from this invasion of the river which was his refuge from daylight and heat, the passage to his nighttime grazing grounds. Water, and the deepening dark in which we could barely see the shaken surface of the river subside, swallowed him up as it did everything else outside the little circle around the fire. The zebras barked and barked; nearby, crickets chirped, and a log blew into flame. A stranger to this earth, I was tired and apprehensive and — in my deep ignorance — helpless. How was it, then, that some unknown, profound part of me felt so blissfully at home?

III

THERE WAS A MIDDAY lull — no wind, nothing moving, a stillness so deep that the gurglings of the river sounded like a symphony, the world felt suspended in clear, golden space. Into this fell from time to time the round flute-notes of two boubou shrike — one bird singing an obbligato, in harmony, to the voice of its mate. Twice, while I rested in the tent under a canopy of leaf shadows, a swarm of bees passed overhead like a flight of planes, making a loud, quickly vanishing roar, emphasizing, as African sounds have a way of doing, the immense quiet. At this time of day the animals, except for the herds grazing out on the plains, rest in the shade of thickets and bush where the air is pleasantly cool and comfortable. Out in the open you are less aware of the sensation of heat than of the sun's solid weight pressing down on top of your head and pushing up, in reflection, from the ground — stay out in it for any length of time without a hat and it is like being squeezed between stones. Bob stood it better than the rest of us and was off somewhere on foot, reconnoitering, leaving us in the grove to our various quiet occupations: Amyas going over camera equipment and Nat studying bird books, Margaret — an embroidery frame propped on her knees — working at a piece of exotic stitchery which looked like a barbaric mask; "I'm going to call it 'Africa'," she said. When we spoke, it was in whispers or very low voices.

Bob had been quite right: already, after only two days, the civilized world seemed not only nonexistent but nearly impossible to envisage. Usual, mundane preoccupations had been completely replaced by the most sensitive attention to cracking twigs, bird voices and animal sounds, to the moving of a branch when there was no wind, to any unusual shape against walls of forest or brush. We had become all awareness, attentiveness, quiet — mixed with more or less fear: acute and heart-pounding the first night when soft and measured footsteps, accompanied by a curious strong smell, woke me out of dreamless sleep and were followed by the huge, wide-spaced splashings of an elephant or a hippopotamus crossing the river. Off and on all that night lions roared, always in pairs, fairly far away, but — were they coming nearer? They sounded like distant thunder which before dying away rolls once more, once more. One lay and listened — a cough from the next tent pricking attention even wider open — trying to fix the direction from which the roaring came, something strangely difficult to do in a tent in the African night. In the morning there were several different opinions. "I'm afraid they're across the river," said Bob, and Margaret and I exchanged relieved glances. The night had been full of mysterious growls, cries, calls, even one horrifying scream, but having once heard a record of

jungle sounds I was braced for them and even stated in the
morning that it had been a fairly quiet night. Bob gave me
an odd look; "You thought so? I thought it was noisy."

We were a curious mixture, those first days, of fear and
bravado, the book knowledge we had brought with us, the
total inexperience we had here. We jumped at a baboon
squawk and went too near bush-covered termite mounds; in

camp we whispered, but on the first trips out in the Land Rover were so excited by game that our voices sent them galloping off. In the African stillness voices carry much as they do in the Arctic so that long before they should have done — since animals don't seem to consider cars alive or in any way threatening — zebras streaked away, drumming the ground; wildebeest, looking like small bearded buffalo, cantered off with ungainly, wooden grace as if they were rocking horses; wart hogs trotted for the woods, tails high and straight as aerials on cars. With impala, the most athletic and graceful of gazelles, our excitement added drama, for the more irrepressible our "ohs" and "look at *that*'s," the higher they leaped, hurtled over one another in their haste to get away, tossed themselves into the air like spray from a fountain.

It was giraffes that taught us to keep the most still. Their combination of shyness and curiosity (rather like our own) sent them ambling off at the slightest stir, but then they stopped to turn and gaze at us in utter immobility out of their wide, heavily lashed eyes. Not even their ears, white on the inside and streaked with black zigzags of lightning, flickered; the furry little horns between stood up like double exclamation marks. Nat, particularly, loved them; when any of us — eyes roving over planes of trees and waves of land — sighted that unmistakable angle and thrust of long necks which, in civilization, one would say were cranes lined up along a pier, his whole being concentrated on getting as near as possible. If one of us whispered too loudly or made a sudden motion, or when eventually we came so close that the giraffe no longer dared stand and stare and finally left, Nat made a little sound of pity and dismay. "I want sometime to get *really* close to one — so I can *commune* with it," he kept saying. Sooner than the rest of us, and in his own direct fashion, Nat longed for what he called confrontations. The word, as he said it, had an impressive, portentous roll.

Margaret looked up from her stitchery and I from my journal; under the tree, Nat's chair stood empty. Had I seen him go? I told her I hadn't. She sighed, got up and looked all around camp, then came back and rejoined me.

"I wish he wouldn't go off by himself," she said. "I don't think he's aware of the dangers, and he isn't very careful — he's not that kind of person."

It was true that earlier that morning he had walked right away from the Land Rover and out into bush as if it were a friend's lawn, and that on a bird walk, the day before, he had hung behind, though Bob, leading us with his rifle, was urging us to keep in a close group.

"You know," she went on, with an uneasy laugh, "He's so enthusiastic and so impulsive; when he gets near water he is likely to fall in!"

"But he *can't,* here!" I protested.

She didn't reply. Perhaps she too was remembering what we had seen yesterday when Bob had been trying to find again a certain dead water, one of the innumerable oxbows left by the river's meandering. After the dazzle of plains, streaming with animals, it had been wonderful to discover this quiet miniature world, screened by big trees, the shallow water starred with water lilies and paved with lily pads. On a dead branch sat a malachite kingfisher — a small enameled statuette which dropped from time to time to catch a fish, returning so rapidly to its perch you were not quite sure you had really seen it happen. Down in the

water a great white egret — whiter-looking than a swan
with its compact plumage and sleek, torpedo-smooth body
— minced with appalling deliberateness after frogs and min-
nows. For over a minute it would hold the most uncom-
fortable-looking pose, then up would come a foot, each
black-thread toe widespread, to be placed with infinite care
in a new position. Here and there "lily-trotters" ran across
the water like comic characters, almost but never quite sinking in, their gait that of people hurrying across hot sand.
Comic in gait, but what plumage! Bodies such a rich and
textured cinnamon brown they seemed made of precious
metal or polished wood; a gray-blue head; the most elegant
black and white striped vests.

But when we tried to find the dead water again, it had
vanished. Up and down along the wall of trees beside the
river we cruised, looking, and at the most likely spot Bob
got out and examined the shoreline, but what he found —
beckoning us to come and see — was something very different. On all fours in the grass behind him, we crept up
a mound on the shore just as a huge hippo came up to us
under its own bow wave and slowly surfaced. It kept on
coming out until it stood free; water poured and dripped
off its scarred hide and collars of fat while it took a long
look at our five heads lined up beside the one clear exit from
the river. With a disgusted grunt it turned away and
waddled out on the other bank and around a curve — all
the time wearing the curious false smile they have, like that
of people who have made it a practice to keep their lips
drawn back no matter what they may be feeling. Four to
five tons of bulk, a huge mouth filled with tusks — they
may not eat meat but they often kill fishermen or anyone

disturbing them. No, it was no place to fall into the water.

Margaret was troubled: she didn't think she could say anything to Nat, and Bob, we had noticed, made no categorical negations unless absolutely necessary; he led us to impose our own restrictions.

"Perhaps Amyas could say something?" She looked at me, needle poised over her embroidery. We were still having a whispered consultation when the red-banded hat came into sight around the trees and the object of our fears sauntered up to us, bird glasses bouncing on his bare chest. His round eyes were shining, his smile contagious.

"I saw a little bird," he said, "green back, yellow throat, rusty breast — beautiful!" After he had gone into the tent, Margaret laughed and lifted her outspread hands. "You see? It's that wonderful enthusiasm of his. In his profession, it's what makes him undertake what others think is impossible."

But before the afternoon was over, our anxiety had spread in another, unlooked-for direction.

Out hunting for buffalo of which Bob had seen a big herd, we came upon our first rhinoceros: a gray rock standing in grass halfway up his sides, a flock of oxpeckers — the birds that live off parasites — riding along his back and neck. He acted very sleepy; we had come within fifty or sixty yards of him before he looked up, then he sensed us and began to charge. Bob veered sharply off and drove away; the grass was too deep, we couldn't get away fast enough. Still he wanted to find the buffalo, which he thought might be in the next big savanna, half hidden by trees. Lines of trees or bush as straight as hedgerows — *dongas* in Swahili — divide the big fields and it can be very hard to find a way around

them. A lot of time had been lost on unsuccessful attempts
when we came to an opening, and a ditch about as wide
as the Land Rover was long. We all got out while Bob
studied it and decided to make a try; the front bumper was
almost up the far rise when the rear end hung and embedded
itself sickeningly into the bank. I looked across, measuring
the height of the farther bank, and in the grass beyond —
burnished deep gold in the late light — saw two great
thorned heads look up from browsing: only seventy-five to

a hundred yards away they couldn't help but hear us. Flinging off jackets, the men set to work jacking up the car,
carrying logs and placing them under the wheels, while Bob
asked Margaret and me to keep a watch on the rhinos and
let him know their movements. If they came? I supposed
we could climb into the Land Rover but remembered a
photograph of a car totally demolished by a charging rhino.
They weigh over a ton; once they start their charge, they run
twenty to thirty miles an hour. Standing there, alternately
watching the rhinos and the work on the car, I became sure
that I heard loud breathing from somewhere quite near,
deep in the grass — louder even than the thumping in my
ears.

At last the car struggled free and with daylight dimming,
the sky full of heavy clouds and smoke from grass fires, we
headed out into the field with the rhinos — there was nowhere else to go. "You watch and tell me what they do,
I'll drive," said Bob.

We came alongside them: they moved toward us in the
deep grass, stood still and considered, moved away toward
the forest. We started home, a very long way around.

"They're not bad, really," Bob assured us; "in captivity
they'll eat out of your hand in three weeks. They are just
stupid — incredibly stupid — and they don't see well, and
they are apt to be unpredictable."

We had been badly frightened and now doubts about our
guide's judgment and about the wisdom of the whole expedi-
tion invaded the hollow which panic had left. I wondered,
for instance, why we had come to this wild area first, and
how sure of him we *were*. What, really, did we know about
him, or about how any of us would act in emergency? What

burst of energy and judgment could I count on in *myself?*
In this landscape and this new life, I didn't yet know who I
was. Part of me, I realized — that part which was fascinated
by seeing the great animals close to — longed for "confrontations," the rest of me was terrified. I wondered if I
would rise to the occasion, for rise it would be, summoning
a sense of self-assurance combined with respect for the animal; acceptance of its dignity yet recognition of my superior
intelligence. Superior? How ridiculous! The animals' intelligence was vastly superior to mine in what counted here
— in quick-wittedness, stealth, awareness of air and terrain
— all that multitudinous frame of reference which we abandoned — how many thousand years ago! Back in camp,
where it was already dark, Margaret and I clung to one another, laughing — with relief, and at our own inconsistency:
we had come all these miles and spent all that money in
order to see the wildlife and here we were, scared to death
in its presence.

But that evening Nat told me he had seen our faces when
we were near the rhinos — "and I was *impressed,*" he added

gravely. And the next day Bob did something which showed that he had indeed been noticing.

Just back from his bath in the washing pools half a mile down the river, hair still shining wet and smoothed down, his eyes were intense with excitement: he had found a big crocodile — he could take us almost to it in the Land Rover. Then he hesitated:

"If you don't mind, we'll take the boys along with us. I like to have them see crocs; it makes them more careful when they go for water."

Crocodiles, huge and armored and accountable for more human deaths than any other African animal, have been hunted so much that they are extremely shy. Middays, they like to come out and sleep in the sun but once frightened they return to the river and may stay submerged for hours, only the periscopes of their snouts lying on the surface, looking like large bubbles or bits of scum. Bob led us to a hollow in the river bank, partially screened by grass. The opening was narrow; we had to crawl one at a time up the slope on hands and knees and then lie flat to have a look.

No one even whispered; Kimani crept up holding his *panga,* the broad, two-edged machete which the Mau Mau used. The "croc" lay in the mud directly across from us — a small island, mottled brown and yellow-green like the surrounding sedge, uneven and blotchy as the earth bank behind; the camouflage was so perfect it was impossible to see where he began and ended. We all had our look, then someone made a noise: at once a knobbed eyelid drew back and the island slid under the water and disappeared, dragging in behind it a tail ridged with spikes like those of a medieval portcullis. It kept on coming and coming. He was fifteen feet long, Bob thought; they seldom get to be more than twenty feet but with age they grow wider and wider: it was easy to understand stories of their dragging even a full-grown rhino or buffalo into the river, clamping a leg in those jaws and holding the victim under until it drowned. They were like river mud become animated and armed, dragging more advanced forms of life back into the ooze. No one, seeing what we had seen, would ever again be careless near water.

When the sun had lowered we went for a walk, Bob in the lead with his rifle. The sound of the shells dropping home, the click of the gun locking, were wonderfully reassuring and on the animal paths we followed through thick bush it was good to stay as close behind him as one could. We were out for birds. Almost at once a tauraco flew up and coasted into a farther tree, the low sun shining through its blood-red wings as if through the petals of a hibiscus; a few trees away perched a trogon — iridescent green with a breast which flashed into flame when he flew from us. The trail ran out at the river's edge and our coming sent a troop of baboons crossing over in front of us — one after another leaping from a fallen log to the down-hanging branch of a tree on the other shore, swinging and scrambling up and vanishing into the forest on the other side. That did it: every bird within hearing went deeper into forest and bush; every small rustling and twittering stopped.

We tried the thickets on the other side of camp and coming up to the river bank, at this point quite high, Bob motioned with his gun for us to drop, laid a finger to his lips. It was so still and we kept so quiet I was sure I heard my heart as I crawled after him through the grass. From the top of the rise the wooded bank opposite us looked like a landscape screen, water swirling around its base, and along the top — partly hidden by leaves — a frieze of elephants moving very slowly along, feeding as they went. They were less than a hundred feet from where, barely breathing, we lay and watched them: one huge bull, a baby whose mother kept it under her trunk, feeding it leafy twigs between bites of her own, five or six others of varying sizes — one couldn't separate enough to count them the gray boulders of their backs — yet even through the leaves one saw the long-drawn-out deliberateness, momentum and at the same time the extreme delicacy of everything they did. Elephants seem to move to a rhythm belonging to other ages, other worlds so old they almost go back to the sea: the trunks — feeling, testing, exploring as though with sight — are like refinements of sea anemones' feelers; the huge, veined ears move as sea fans do in the underwater swell. They made no sound as they shifted positions, walked across a clear space and on into the forest but the cracking and ripping of branches sounded like a lot of foresters at work. Farther

into the forest we heard more rustlings and snappings: they
must have been part of a much larger herd.

Creeping through thickets, not making the slightest noise,
I felt terribly uneasy. At the rate we moved it was impossible
to watch the path for snakes and at the same time examine
bushes for hidden animals — which, even with Bob in front,
seemed to me vitally necessary. At any second I expected a
leopard or rhino or buffalo to come charging out and
mightn't he do so after the first of the party passed by?
Every atavistic terror of being jumped on quickened in my
veins; my skin became remarkably alive. What a relief,
after watching the elephants, to sit quietly on a high grassy
mound at a bend in the river — looking out over miles of
plains and down two arms of the river, one noisy with rapids,
the other wide and placid, and in front of us a giant fig tree
alive with baboons and with two green pigeons in its crown.
The sun was setting; with prolonged rustlings of leaves and
chattering exchange, the baboons were settling for the night.
Like children playing "I'm the king of the castle," two of
them climbed to the very top of the tree, sending the
pigeons off and away, then sat down side by side facing the
sunset — two coppery statues against a deepening turquoise
sky.

Over dinner under the stars we talked little about the
day; we had lived and shared it so fully it was easy to let it
go into the past. We were still getting to know one another
that first week and most of the talk was about our families,
the projects and enterprises we had left on coming away,
people we knew. Though we felt so far removed and were
rapidly changing our whole way of being (more so than we
yet recognized), we still put out those usual bridges across

gaps — counting on them to take us across, forgetting how flimsy they can be, how they may even fail to be connections at all but uncrossable moats. Bob, sharing none of our common background, had little to add; he told us instead about the Masai and other tribes he knew, about the wonderful things he had seen on trips to Lake Rudolf and through Ethiopia, about things he had read. He was a great reader and had a whole box of books with him; long after we were asleep and the boys' voices had run out into silence, his tent glowed from the lamp inside.

The rest of us were in bed by nine, exhausted as children. Each day was so full, we lived at so many different levels of experience, in so many variations of the basic, natural rhythm we had fallen into, that time completely altered its nature, becoming once more as it was when one was a child. Instead of bracing against its rush as though in a spate of water dragging at your legs, you stood at a calm center, possibilities stretching out in every direction. Sidereal time, near the Equator, is equally divided into twelve hours of darkness, twelve of light. (The Swahili way of measuring it is to call seven o'clock — the first hour of daylight — one; eight is two and the same goes for the hours of the night.) Even when I was asleep, the nights felt strangely long. Awake, I lay and listened to the unfamiliar and eerie sounds, trying to identify them; was filled sometimes by sheer, irrational terror as I was when a child, as my far-off ancestors must have been every time the sun went down and they huddled in a cave or around a fire. Each night's sounds were different. The first it was hippos, zebra and lions; the next, one persistent wailing hyena and the anguished barks of baboons; another, wind and showers drowned out animal voices till toward morning when four lions tuned up, roaring back and forth to one another. Strangely, the greater quiet felt more threatening than the noises had: I suffered more misgivings from what I didn't hear than what I did.

After this kind of atavistic alertness and the sheer length of hours of darkness, nothing was sweeter than the first notes of bird song, the first warm glow in the sky above the river, casting fig and palm trees into silhouette and laying their black reflections on the water. A few feathers of cloud caught light; the bird flutings and reiterated phrases increased. Outside the tent we would hear Njorogi's soft cough and a gentle little clatter as he brought things for morning tea. If he hadn't heard us stirring, he scratched on the canvas — just beginning now to grow translucent. Rather quietly and hastily we all greeted one another and compared notes about the night, drinking our hot tea around the table set in the dewy grass, hurrying to get off in the Land Rover before sunup. Then came the steady, slow cruising across savanna and plain, through grass deep enough to brush the car's hood or over cropped and burned turf as flat as a lawn; along and across mazes of animal paths printed into the ground by thousands of hooves; between thorn trees and along forest edges scalloped with dark openings where paths led in and anything might come out. In half a mile the scenery might change completely: turn from a cultivated park to an overgrown orchard; grow hummocks and lush grass and thickets that looked like swamps yet were as hard as concrete; give us great peaceful views out over surrounding country — always with the high escarpment to the west. Sometimes it shrank into dead pockets of dry thorn, spiky grass and high termite mounds, a sort of devil's playground.

For two or three hours we cruised — no destination before us — our car rocking along. In the open hatch over the back seat three of us stood as on the deck of a ship, the air flowing past as cool as water, and looked out for any shape or movement of interest. The number of two-eared stumps and hulking mounds we took for animals was amazing; it was nearly always Bob who, while avoiding pits and mounds, mud wallows and scraping trees, murmured "There's a harrier eagle," "Two jackal off there to the left" — long before we saw anything at all. Excursions were a mixture of leisurely exploration, keenest searching, held-breath anticipation and deep excitement — the only certainty about them being their surprises. Even knowing the location of camp and outlying landmarks, there was no guessing what impassable terrain might lie between; every time we went out was a fresh adventure in which we were coexplorers.

Afterwards we came back to enormous hearty break-
fasts and went about the small tasks of the day, a great
sense of peace and tranquility over all of us. Around the
cook fire there was a continuous running of voices and low
laughter like the voices of the river. On a tree opposite
camp two little bee-eaters (Nat's green-backed and yel-
low-throated birds) perched close together, darting straight
up to snatch a moth or bug, dropping back to their branch
to gobble it up; they seemed to enjoy staying near us.
At such times it was the gentlest and most inviting of
landscapes. Soft puffy clouds drifted overhead, the air
was full of sweetness and the unmistakable pungency it
has in Africa; around the campsite the river wound and
dimpled, birds called and sang. Then a branch cracked
or a tree fell: elephants. Or suddenly an unholy hulla-
baloo like that of a dog fight mixed with coyote howls
broke out where baboons were squabbling — and with some
last whimpers and squeals, one baboon raced out of the
forest into the clearing, glancing back over his shoulder with
a sad, injured look. Monkeys in zoos, particularly baboons,
are such embarrassing and repellent caricatures of ourselves,
the expression in their eyes so nearly human and yet clearly
not, that they can be very disquieting; here, maybe because
of all the animals they were most nearly like us, we found
them endearing. Their evening family hour enchanted us:
the children boxing and wrestling, the parents sitting about
nibbling at grass or scratching an itch, couples fondly and
attentively grooming one another, and a huge old grandfather in the background like a president at a Board Meeting. We smiled indulgently at our camp jesters, perhaps
partly for giving us back a little of the vanishing self-im-

portance to which we still clung. For what *were* we out here in all this immensity but fascinated and awed and help-less outsiders? Bob had become part of his surroundings at once; he had moved somewhere away from us and we had not caught up. Beyond our little group he doubted that there was anyone between us and Narok but the Masai, and the last signs of *them* were the opalescent clouds from their fires, dying away now far to the east. Then one day he found a human footprint in the sand upriver from us, nearer the Escarpment. "People!" he said, with a mock horror which something inside me echoed. I didn't want "people"; I didn't want anything; I felt as if, just created and waking from the long and curious dreams of our other lives, we were the only humans on this beautiful earth we had been given. With a leap of the heart I knew us as one expression of the same joy.

IV

ON THE FIFTH DAY, we broke camp and moved, nostalgic at leaving the site we had come to know, hypercritical on arrival at the new one. It takes much less than we think to make a place our own — less time, fewer things. Laurens van der Post describes the wife of a Kalahari bushman smoothing the sand under a bush for a bed and laying out her ostrich shell water flasks and cooking things with all the grace of a woman arranging a whole room — probably with all the pleasure too, since that particular enjoyment can stretch only so far, beyond a certain point becoming a web in which we are caught or else we no longer see our own possessions.

At each camp our tents were set up for us and beds put together and made, but deciding where to hang jackets, hats and binoculars and store our books and gear, tying the mirror on the frame of the tent fly, in the best light, at a height that would do for both of us — this was making it home. Each camp was different — its view, the disposition of tents, the terrain. The surface under the ground-sheet might be smooth as a floor or lumpy and veined with roots; our shade from the equatorial sun of every thickness and design from the delicate net of bare twigs on a flat-topped acacia to the sixty-foot rustling wave of leaves on a wild fig tree; at Amboseli the tent walls became plastered with tenacious clusters of grass-heads in crazy posterlike patterns — it was all the same: we became fond of each home in turn. In a much shorter time than it takes to remember the light switches in a new apartment, our hands knew where to find things in the dark, feet memorized the turnings of the way to the toilet tent, and when rain kept us inside the pattering canvas and we rearranged everything so that the five of us could fit in for drinks and dinner around one small table, it was like playing house as children on stormy afternoons. Always, on breaking camp, there was a little wrench at seeing everything dismantled and packed into duffels and then driving off to an unknown destination.

Our second camp, across the river, was no more than ten miles away but because the river was high and must be crossed at the one bridge, we had to go in a great L to get there, driving back to the foot of the Escarpment and along the track at its base which we had left so long ago. From a few miles west of our first camp the grassland rose gently all the way to the Escarpment itself and that morning the whole slope was brushed into waves by the wind. Near where the steep, rough rise began and the tall grass ended, we got out and lay in it, as out of sight in its deep warmth as the five lions we saw on the way in, surrounded by the continuous singing hiss of the wind passing through it — like the hiss of foam far out at sea. On the Land Rover's hood

Bob stood having a look around: up against the mountain
— looking like a brown wreath tilted toward us, he found a
Masai *boma,* the thorn hedge with which they enclose their
cattle and huts; he thought it seemed inhabited and worth
a visit. From nearer we saw what a magnificent location it
had — back against the mountainside and with a view south-
ward over the immense lands stretching down into Tanganyika. Near the entrance a single candelabra euphorbia,
big and widespread as an old oak, held up multiple green
arms. Two figures stood beside it with their backs to the
village, watching us approach — tall, holding taller spears,
earth-brown capes flapping around their long legs. With the
engine in low we climbed slowly up toward them. From
somewhere very far back in time I felt that I knew those
figures — armed and motionless and still: they were the
archetypal sentinels who had protected villages, then the
citadels and megarons of Greece — like eyries on their rocky
hills; who, in the Middle Ages, had stood on battlements
and watchtowers, fingering their arrows as unidentified
horsemen swam up out of the distance. It was a solemn
feeling, advancing into their fateful presence. Then we saw
the brilliant whiteness of the smiles in their dark faces and
they were walking forward and in another minute were
greeting us. *Jambo* has an important sound, like plucking
the strings of a bass viol — it is worthy of the occasion of
saluting strangers — and the way they said it, and shook our
hands, it was clear they valued our coming. Now they were
joined by two or three younger men and several women
and children — the girls' necks encircled with concentric
rings of small brightly colored beads, arms heavily brace-
leted and everyone's ears — men's, women's and children's

— distorted and festooned with earrings hanging down to
their shoulders. They all came out through an opening in the
thorn fence and gathered around us and this time we were
more prepared to meet them: we indicated in sign language
how beautiful we found their view and their entrance tree;
we laid our hands on top of the children's heads, which is
their way of greeting children. One child ducked away from
under my hand and two of the men gave embarrassed laughs
and apologized for his bad manners. The child smiled and
slipped over between them, half hiding, and one of the men
laid an arm around him.

We went into the village through one of the openings in
the hedge which was at least six feet thick — made of two
fences of saplings driven into the ground, the space between
them filled in solidly with brush. Bob patted it as he walked
through, saying *"Hapana simba"* — no lion — could get in
here. Our hosts liked this and laughed with pleasure. Right
inside the entrance lay a pile of branches which they
dragged across the opening at night to wall themselves and
their cattle in — so big we had to walk around it to get inside. The herds were all out with their herdsmen so that
the boma seemed quite deserted; there were only six huts
in it but they were finely constructed: plastered with dried
dung on the inside, then a stuffing of grass and, on the outside, upright sticks bound close together with some kind of
tough grass. The roofs, also of dung, were very pleasant to
touch: dry and light and firm — rather like a thick felt. The
one I went into had a sort of vestibule in which stood several spears, then a little boxed-in stall with a gate across it
like a baby's gate, in which lay a newborn calf, long legs
tucked under, its enormous eyes mild and startled. Bending

down, for the hut was no more than five feet high, I went on around a corner to where in the inside room I could just make out the tiny figure of an unbelievably old-looking woman — an upright, smoked mummy leaning on a stick.

When I was back outdoors the prettiest and youngest woman in the group ducked into her house and came out carrying a fat and sleepy baby about two months old to show to us, careful to have us see his fine little balls. He screwed up his face at the bright light and started to cry and she slipped a breast out of her cape and put it into his mouth. Noticing that his bottom was soiled she wiped it with a piece of paper — from where? — it looked like a bit of wrapping paper from a cracker box. With the baby quiet at her breast we could see how she had decked it out with little anklets of tiny red beads and a single circle of white beads around the belly; curled up in her arms the child looked like a beautiful figure of bronze. Loveliest of all were its rings — one on each middle finger with a bridle leading to a bracelet so that they couldn't come off — made of the smallest brightest colored beads and one white cowrie shell at the center.

Everyone in the place was charming, courteous, sensitive; the faces were very intelligent. I gave the children and their mothers and grandmothers some chewing gum, explaining in sign language that they mustn't swallow it though they seemed to know this already. The men were deeply interested in the binoculars hung around my neck so I took them off and they looked through them — out toward the plains — eagerly discussing what they saw, handing them back with broad grins and much show of gratitude. Bob had told us how totally unacquisitive they are, their entire lives centered on the cattle which are their food, drink, building material and covering. Living on milk they need no water; for strength they add cows' blood, extracted much as we get blood for a sample, a thong tied around the animal's neck till the jugular stands out, then an arrow (with a stop on it) shot at close range and the blood drawn off and beaten with a whisk till it coagulates into a kind of curd. Cow urine is used as a cleansing and disinfectant agent; before milking they wash their hands in it. The young warriors eat meat but most of the cattle die of old age and are skinned for the hides. Even the youngest children are aware of the wealth of cattle and play games of pretend herds with sticks and stones; we found a little pile of such counters in front of a doorway. No need for refrigerators, stoves, money or possessions — their cattle are all of these and all they seem to want so that, as yet, almost none show any interest in adopting our way of living, and many are very sorry for us. Out of the few who have gone as far as Nairobi or have studied at universities, most cannot wait to get back to the mud villages, the miles of walking over heat-shimmering country beside their herds.

Coming from our world of continually accelerating change and complexity in every aspect of our lives — into theirs so perfectly and timelessly tuned to their surroundings, I felt warmed and lighthearted. They are certainly not Rousseau's Noble Savage — like the early settlers of our old West, they raid one another's herds and have sharp battles and those who have had accidents or deeply infected eyes are crippled and go blind, but on the other hand their faces are not clouded with the anxieties and guilts and harassments of ours. It is a marvelous thing to see a naturally proud human face; one has to go farther and farther to find that unmistakable look in the eye. Did all Neolithic people have it? Or are these people — whose ancestors came south from the Nile valley, adding Ethiopian and other blood to the Nilotic — a remnant who hit upon a specially beneficent existence? One finds among them a great variety of facial types — some who have just stepped out of Egyptian paintings and others with black skins and Negroid features, a few with high cheekbones and slant eyes — but they all stand, and move, like royalty. It is a great sight to come upon them striding along in the dust, their long, slender legs covering the ground fast and smoothly, their togas flying back, and have them, instead of wave, hold up a hand with the palm toward you, the fingers together. It is a grand, free gesture; it has the dignity of the blessing bestowed by saints in Byzantine mosaics.

Already this particular village may have been abandoned for a new one, built like a bird's nest on some other hill, its occupants having moved on; in another year, then, there will scarcely be a vestige of the one we saw. We walked out through its thorn hedge to our car standing in the deep shade of the euphorbia tree, our hosts escorting us all the way, and a great wave of "the pity beyond all telling" swept over me. This has happened to me often when leaving a person or place I cared for and am unlikely ever to see again, and this concurrence was one that could never be repeated: the great bright distances now beginning to quiver with heat while our high vantage point was still swept by the morning's cool wind; all those shining bronze and copper and black faces around us, in their extravagantly vivid settings of earrings and necklaces; the hearty smiles and the soft voices saying *Sere, sere* — farewell, farewell. Something, one felt, must remain from what was extended there between us. For several minutes as we bumped downhill over the rough ground to the track below, the dark figures remained where they were, following our descent.

We drove back toward Narok through the burned land, crossed the river and branched off onto another smaller track leading down to Tanganyika, then cutting across open savannas returned once more to the winding green line of forest along the river. Although it was not yet one o'clock when we reached our new campsite, the morning had already been a day in itself. Often, like that, we lived three or four days in one and now were happy to sit in the chairs which were the first things to be unloaded and look about at our new surroundings while baboons ambled out of the woods, walking on the backs of their hands, and looked at us. The place was like a park — big, widely spaced trees, a very tidy meadow and, beyond a far line of trees, the open plains. The river at this point had higher, more impressive banks but no curve encircling us with the partial moat of our other camp. On either side of where the tents were being put up, deep forest came to within a hundred feet; it felt much less protected. And we were out for lions here — particularly for the big pride Bob had found on his last trip! Even though it was to be a hard search, we began seeing individual ones almost at once.

That afternoon, near the edge of the forest, we came to a clear pool framed in rich grass from which a herd of impala and little Thomson's gazelles were drinking while others, nearby, licked at one of the patches of bare ground which

yield the salt and minerals the animals need. The drinking
ones drove ripples across their images in the floating sky;
behind them others stood waiting their turn, the late light
accentuating the clear black web of lines on the white linings
of their ears, singling out long legs and lyrate horns with all
the delicacy of Persian or Indian miniatures. For a long time
we sat quietly watching them. Animals at water are a moving sight for no matter how great their number, they line
up without crowding behind the one drinking who, as soon
as he has finished, gets away as quickly as possible to make
room for the next: it is as orderly as communicants at the
altar rail; it gives you the odd sense that water, to them,
comes close to being a deity. (At our first camp we had
seen wildebeest approach a water hole in a line that ran for
at least a mile out into the plain — hundreds plodding patiently single file or standing bunched up like marchers in
a parade which is held up by unseen delays up front.) This
one-at-a-time and no-lingering behavior suggests a fear of
lurking predators, yet attacks at water holes are very rare —
as though the animals all felt equally respectful and vulnerable there.

While we were watching, Bob had noticed far off a tree
full of vultures and we drove over to have a look, for vultures, whether in groups or flying in a very straight and pur-
poseful way (most of all, several converging from different
directions), point to a kill as surely as a compass needle.
Near the tree was a high grass mound and right on top of it,
as if on a dais, lay a lioness with two big cubs. How proud
she looked! How indifferent to us! Bob was uncertain,
though, whether she was one of the pride or not; he didn't
recognize her. We couldn't see what she was guarding but,

waiting off to one side in a pompous, deferential group, stood a dozen marabou storks, tail-coated and solemn as undertakers, and more vultures than could be counted — all headed one way like filings to a magnet, sharp faces peering from their huddled witch-capes. Very gently we came up till we were the length of a long living-room away and Amyas stood up in the open hatch, photographing, but the lioness

only looked the other way with uttermost disdain. One of the cubs stared and stared at us, the other peeked shyly over his mother's back. Finally — had she heard a whisper, or a shutter click? — the lioness suddenly looked straight at us, switched her tail and growled. We drove away, amazed at how close she had let us come — with a kill *and* cubs? But put one foot to the ground, Bob said . . . it would be another story.

Oh, we were on the right side of the river now for lions! Off and on all night we heard their roars — an earth-shaking sound more elemental than vocal, much nearer than before. Also (as usually happened the first night in any new camp), it seemed every animal for miles around came to investigate. Baboons screamed and barked and hyenas wailed like sirens but noisiest of all were the elephants who ripped off branches and toppled trees so continuously and so close that it was like being in the middle of a lumbering operation. I lay, listening, wondering if they were coming right into camp, heart pounding, and when I heard Amyas was awake too I reached across the dark and held on to his hand. It could be that the herd we'd seen on the other side of the river had now come over here — they often travel thirty miles a day — and there were we, in bed, on the ground: with awful vividness my mind reran whole scenes from African movies of elephants stampeding. Cracks, sharp as pistol shots, now alternated with great branchy rustles, thumps and long-drawn-out ripping sounds, occasionally the slow crescendo of a whole big tree coming down. Then footsteps and Bob's voice: "Is anyone awake?" Was it time to get up? No light shone through the canvas and the moon having set, our tent was dark as a cellar.

"Those elephants are rather close." (Even at this hour his words were gently clipped.) "I think it might pay to let them know we're here." I remembered that the wind, here, blew across the campsite and unless it grew shifty, which it seldom did, they couldn't get our scent.

We unzippered the tent and came out to find him, rifle in hand, looking toward the woods a hundred feet beyond. We flashed light on the wall of foliage but saw nothing. He began talking in a very loud voice and we all joined in — a ridiculous imitation of a noisy cocktail party. "Shall we sing?" I asked, "or make a racket?"

"I wouldn't like to risk annoying them," he replied. "Let's hope they'll leave now."

The crashing went a little farther away but not much. Before morning the sound was added to by the triple rasping growl of a leopard, so closely followed by baboon barks that it all seemed one sound and, in fact, might have been since baboons mimic leopards most cleverly in order to warn the tribe.

The dawn, when it finally came, made one want to worship. The early morning light, so beautiful everywhere on earth, has in Africa the look of the very first day: there is a radiance, a sweetness, a richness to it streaming over the golden grass that makes it almost palpable; the animals standing about on the plains are sculptured by it into living statues; the grasses are turned into shimmering molten wire. I said something of this to Bob over tea and he laughed: "Yes, and you're so glad to have made it once again through to daylight!"

"Well, aren't you?"

"Of course. Sometimes, out here, I'm scared stiff."

"Bob, if elephants *do* come into camp at night, what happens?"

"They feel in front of them with their trunks."

"So when they feel tents they'll go away again?"

"Probably."

They would respect camp as being our territory, he added, and told how on another safari elephants had passed within ten feet of a sleeper's tent — they found the tracks in the morning. If *we* approached *them*, they would be more aggressive and would probably warn us off with rushes and trumpeting. Even then it would probably be just a show, for animals simply don't want to engage in hostilities: it's too dangerous, they are too likely to get hurt. No hospitals, no Blue Cross, Amyas put in. Bob smiled, finished his tea, and standing up, hands in the pockets of his old green jacket, said: "Well, shall we go and look for the lions?"

We were on high land several miles above camp and the sun was just up when we met not lions but wildebeest — thousands upon thousands plodding through the radiant grass single file, along the innumerable winding paths they beat into the ground. At our coming they broke into their oddly wooden gait, sometimes stretching out into an all-out run, the sun shining now through their streaming, fringed beards and turning them softly silver; on others, going past at a different angle, turning the vertical stripings on their shoulders vivid black, making them look like wrinkled old men.

We stopped the car and turned off the motor: we were in the middle of a migration. On our left, an unbroken frieze of animals, like a procession in a cave painting, wound away behind us; on our right, a similar line plodded and loped off that way: we were the rock around which the stream divided. Both lines, coming toward us over a rise of ground, were being continuously replenished from a reservoir of creatures ahead and below — this reservoir, in turn, being added to by huge herds trickling into it from across as many plains as were in view.

"It's like watching life being created and pouring out of the earth's womb," Nat whispered, his face solemn under the curly brim of his hat.

An occasional bawl sounded over the muffled drumming of the ground and the rustle of wind in grass, otherwise the procession went on in orderly silence. Who, or what, had started it? What authority brought about all at once that patient submission, leading every small isolated herd to join the whole and keep driving toward new pastures? Seeing it, one almost felt a special wildebeest "soul," the all-but-visible commanding, coordinating force which was their immortal guide.

But then we left the life-teeming plains for a still higher ridge, and moved almost at once into a terrible dead land, so thick with leafless trees bristling with two-inch whistling thorns that when they closed in behind, on all sides and in front of us, it felt as sinister as entering an enormous trap. There was nothing to do but weave through them like a shuttle in a loom, letting them scrape the sides of the car and snap back into place behind or mow them straight down and have them clatter along underneath. Windows screwed up, we sat as if in punishment, depressed now as we had been elated before, seeing no life whatever, beginning to feel the heat, having nothing to say, until as unexpectedly as it had begun the purgatorial land ended and we were out again in gold grass with here and there a flat-topped acacia, held up on the ribs of its branches like a Japanese umbrella.

Sometimes it seemed as if the Land Rover, like a Western pony, decided where it wanted to go. Now it veered from the obvious way and climbed a rise where a clump of trees with rocks and grass underneath laid deep shade. Everything under the trees was dappled white and buff and dark brown. There was no wind but still the dapples moved, grew paired ears and triangular faces turned our way, finally sorted themselves out into a lioness with four cubs: even with nothing between us and them they were scarcely distinguishable from their mottled bed. The cubs were in a half-sleepy, half-playful state; white bellies very full, they lolled on their backs, and rolled over lazily, an outsized paw flinging up and flopping along the side of a rock, a tail flicking. The mother sat a little away from them, sideways to us, utterly aloof. Her disdain was humiliating: didn't she know we were *there*? Didn't she care? She lifted her long proud head to sniff the wind, the great squared-off jaw given a further lift by the thicker white fur below it, and ignored us completely, while one cub broke away and moved down through reeds to a blue pool where he drank and drank. According to Amyas' focus-finder this was fifty feet from where we sat in the car, photographing, seeing all the lions so clearly in our glasses we could almost feel the soft fuzzy fur and look deep into their light-filled clear gold eyes. The eyebrows, like small brown leaves, were set at an angle above, giving them a very young, a very quizzical expression.

"Are *they* yours, Bob?"

"Hard to tell. She may be one of them and may just like

this place for the day — in which case she'll probably join up again when they start roaring tonight."

"How big did you say the pride was?"

"About twenty. You know you do find lone lionesses, but she would be exceptional to have brought up four healthy cubs to that size without help." We looked at her with new admiration.

Life in the wilds, as every camper knows, offers all the vivid contrasts of event and mood which civilized life covers up or avoids, and in Africa, where the contrasts of temperature and terrain are so extreme, your presence so infinitesimal, you may be swung several times a day between heaven and hell. The morning's scenes were still spreading contentment in us when we drove off upriver in the afternoon to bathe at a waterfall Bob knew and thought we could get to in spite of the fires, still smoldering on, though he feared we might have some trouble. We had enough trouble so that you asked yourself why, when you could have stayed comfortably at home, you ever came to this impossible, horrible continent. Baking in the solid glare of early afternoon we rocked and bumped through miles of burn, an infernal region of scorched earth throwing up ash at us as we passed through it, elephant-tortured trees, smoking logs and stumps, rocks. When Bob tried to get the Land Rover across a rocky ditch in which it seemed certain the transmission would break, we suggested it might be better to bathe where we did yesterday, but he wanted to try one more way. We had been hunting for the waterfall an hour when even *his* perseverance gave out and he took us to another stretch of river he knew where we might at least fish since the bathing was only fair — the water deep enough for crocodiles.

There wasn't enough wind there to stir a blade of grass; shade was in unsafe bush or on ground strewn with the tattered debris of palm fronds, broken-off branches, elephant droppings big around as flour canisters; flies — not the soft clinging kind the Masai don't even bother to brush away, but loud and biting ones — were everywhere except the sunniest places. I settled for one of those — a hump of a little peninsula where nothing could come out of the bush without my seeing it, and with hat well down, hands smeared with fly dope, set about writing in my journal. Farther upstream Margaret silently stitched away at one of the eyes on her African mask — filling in the round space with dizzy black and white circles like some kind of voodoo target. The men fished. From where I sat I could watch Amyas cast out into the muddy coils of the river and slowly tease the lure back in with delicate little jerks. He is an experienced fisherman and it was beautiful to watch him — his whole body in tune with the river's current and the movement of the lure across it: he was thinking and feeling and *being* fish. When he got one on and the rod curved into a bow and he walked up and down on the shore gouged by big animal footprints, reeling in, playing out, talking quietly to himself so as to keep steady, Bob came and offered to help if he needed it for we had no net and the crocs meant we couldn't go in after the fish. It was a fine catfish, ugly as sin, with the whiskers collapsing all around its face — feeling for the element that wasn't there — and with a heavy strong body which it was a wonder to have held by the lightly hooked lip. Farther upstream Nat caught one too, and Amyas had another and called me to come and stand by. Climbing down from my scorching perch, careful not to

trip on muddy roots or turn my ankle in elephant holes —
and at a place where the bank slid off very steeply into deep
water, not to fall in — I thought how out of our irritable
and enervated state the afternoon had been saved. By the
time we left that stretch of river — and returned to the Land
Rover, where a lot of zebra were waiting for it to go away
so that they could get down to drink — I was almost fond of
the place in all its impossibility.

Kimani skinned and cut the fish into chunks and served
it with little new potatoes in a sauce as smooth and subtle as
any of us had ever tasted. The tables, that night, were set
out in the open, near the campfire and away from trees and
tents. Over the forest on the far side of the river the half-
moon lay on its back; barely clear of the trees behind the
cook fire hung the Southern Cross — a kite streaming off
westward — and in the east, where the horizon was far
away, the stars shone clear down to the ground. I looked
up at Venus, beginning to set, and there beside it — yes, it
was: a satellite, rolling along eastward, steady and purpose-
ful, going past all the millions of transfixed stars. Bob ran
and got the boys and they hurried out into the clearing; in
the roll of soft Kikuyu words I heard "Americaner" and
"photographer." "They understand about them all right," he
said, returning, "they ask if there are men in it, or cameras."

Njorogi brought more stew; the meat of the catfish was
smooth and firm and tender.

"I wonder how many people on other worlds out there are
eating catfish under the stars."

"Plenty, probably."

"Did you see that Hoyle, the physicist, thinks the most
important thing scientists have to do is to learn to communi-

cate with life elsewhere, since it's unlikely we'll get there
ourselves?"

"They might be way ahead of us."

"Strange thought . . ."

"I wonder what kind of a God they have . . ."

How easy and natural there under the sky, no other people
but our Masai friends in all those miles, to talk about religion
and what we believed! Here, orthodoxy, and dogma and all
those club rules over which the different sects had niggling
arguments and sometimes bloody wars, seemed more irrelevant than ever. What did they accomplish but bewilder-
ment, division, hostility? It seemed suddenly so simple:
God *was* the Cosmos; was Creation; was Consciousness.
What was there, all around us here, *except* God? God looking out from the eyes of a lion, the gaze of a giraffe; moving
the migrating herds, leading them, one at a time, to water?
Religion was the sky over us, there overhead; it was the
earth at our feet and the blood in our veins; it was the air
we were taking into our lungs, so sheer and revivifying you
felt you could live on it alone and never grow old.

Each day, now, we spoke less and less about what we did
and had and knew about back there at home. What good
were they here? What good was it, for that matter, trying
to please or impress or entertain one another — making any
of the efforts habitually resorted to out of fear of being lost
and unnoticed — of being nobody? Or, worse still, *feeling*
one was nobody — wasn't even there? All of a sudden, the
little story that had to be told, the bright remark waiting for
a silence in order to get spoken (all the while plucking the
sleeve of one's attention, being outrageously distracting)
seemed no more than the supersonic squeaking of bats in

the dark. Say something! Make a noise, so that the bouncing echoes will tell you where, and who, you are! Alone together in this primeval silence, that noise-making was too absurd; we were utterly plain to one another, and growing daily more naked and transparent. One by one the disguises and trappings of civilization, the images we had of ourselves were being stripped off and we watched them go. More and more *we* "let go," wondering what all the effort one usually made was about. The relief was indescribable.

Yet at the same time (though I don't know about the others) a curious crisis was taking place in me. Neither pleasant nor unpleasant, it was simply *there:* a gale in the sky, a preposterous, unidentifiable force. I shook with the appearance of love. Twice, in the companionable midday violence and strangeness of it, as I had once shaken at the peace in camp (not, as might be expected, in the black stillness) I had discovered I was actually trembling. What on earth was happening? I had never felt better so it couldn't be malaria; usually quite a worrier, I had nothing whatever on my mind. It was as though everything I had previously felt as being "me" was being torn loose: I was losing my usual sense of "I." With an objectivity that surprised me, I commanded myself — just as one might do to a companion on a mountaintop, in a storm — to stay still till the gale passed.

Bob, meanwhile, during this talk of religion, said very little — not, it seemed to me, out of criticism or preoccupation but because he had already done that shedding we were doing: he was there where we were going. Well read and well traveled, he was, one felt, equally at home with things he knew about, places he had been to and wherever he was at the moment. You had only to walk with him a little way into the forest, as I had that morning, to feel how centered he was and how aware of everything — from a parasitic fig tree rooted twenty feet over our heads on the trunk of another tree to a spider, almost invisible in a Jack-in-the-beanstalk tangle of weeds — an armored little knot of life no bigger than an autumn bur.

The talk wound, curved, doubled back on itself and left dead waters like the Mara River itself. Amyas, in the middle of a story and looking at the stars, interrupted himself with a stupefied: "Look at the Heavenly Twins . . . my God, there are *three!*" And it was another satellite, this one much higher and slower-moving so that we watched it for what felt like a long time before it went from view only a few degrees above the horizon. Two satellites in one evening, here, over Africa! We felt it as some kind of omen. Bob didn't like them; "Such technology," he said, his chin on his chest, "what will it be like here in fifty years?"

Next morning the men got up before daybreak as usual to hunt for Bob's lions but Margaret and I stayed behind. Waking in my own time, standing for a while at the river's edge, watching birds, I realized I had entered an entirely different state of being, unlike anything ever experienced before, in which I felt extraordinarily light, and peaceful, unpressed by either time or thought— as easy as the early morning air. Greeting Kimani at the cook fire and drinking my coffee out under the sky in the delicate freshness, straightening out the tent, even brushing my teeth, were all gently savored, took place in their own quiet rhythm instead of being gone through on the way to something else. The gale had gone by.

There was no sound from Margaret, still asleep in her tent; I set a chair out on the river bank facing the trees where boubou shrike were fluting together and sat there, prodigally enveloped and invaded by light and warmth and multiple small sounds, caught by the blinding prismatic colors of dew flashing from the grass, swept along on clouds moving in unbroken procession westward in the earth's wake. It has fascinated me before, how, in giving yourself over to your surroundings completely, they are no longer separate from you: you are no longer only yourself but all that, too. A marvelous simultaneous transformation comes over you and the world around you: the dew on the weeds, the calling bird, the tree thrusting into the sky seem at once closer and more extraordinary than ever; the chattering jiggle of thought stopped and "one thought not arising, the real appears." This can happen anywhere, but here, because of our greater attentiveness, our way of living so intensely in the present and moving continually ahead into the next unpredictable adventure, it was almost overwhelming. Was this to be the product of our days, so huge and full and rich with surprises? Of the nights which concealed advancing elephants and the leopard who might be circling the tent — all the known threats which accumulated into others more formidable still for being unknown, lurking just beyond the level of consciousness?

For this morning I was calm and utterly happy as though I had found my place in this oldest of worlds and by accepting it wholly had been taken into its embrace. Accepted — what? Its total insecurity. I now felt I could face anything including dying; then, giving up to the unknown, giving over where there was no responsibility to take, letting go — all those lesser deaths made for more abundant life.

We have gone so far toward managing the world around us that the illusion of controlling fate itself, and of having a specific for every ill but the last one, is almost complete. In the world we had left behind you always felt you could "do something about it"; here you didn't, for although a few things were in our control, many others were no more so than the lightning flickering over the far wall of the Escarpment. Surrounded by the most abundant and varied life still existing on earth, we were equally surrounded by the imminence of death. It was everywhere — in the river, in crocodiles' jaws; in trees and grass and mud — in the snakes we never saw but which were nonetheless there with the deadly drugs, the perfect hypodermic needles with which to put one to sleep forever; in the drive and tonnage and horns of rhino and buffalo and elephants, the uncoiling rush and curved claws of the great cats. We were living in the middle of a life-and-death dance in which the least tick and new shoot of grass was engaged. It was like the figures of Shiva, dancing, his multiple arms and feet flying, one of them holding the drum of creation which summons being out of not-being, another flourishing a flame — the fiery tip of destruction. It made fate as visible as the network of animal paths across the plains — wandering here, there, meeting, converging, crossing. If the wildebeest hadn't turned at this point, but gone the other way instead, he would still be feeding on grass and not fed on by lions; if we had not come along in the Land Rover just when we did yesterday, that third zebra racing along the donga would have been caught by the lion we saw, rampant, about to make its spring. In civilization we know this too, when we miss being hit by a car or land safely in a jet in the fog, but here there was nothing else except what was living and dying and that knowledge got into your heartbeat, your viscera, your skin. And this morning, because I didn't only know it but was learning the steps of that life-and-death dance, I was gay and at peace. There was nothing that had to be done, nowhere to go: I was there — and if that sounds absurd, still it must stand, for quite one of the oddest facts about our world is how little we seem to feel we *are* "there."

All this reflection took place, I suppose, in a very brief time for Margaret, who now came to join me, had heard me pass by her tent on my way to the river bank. She looked unusually radiant. "It's very strange," she said, "but I feel so differently about everything this morning!"

We were still sitting talking, wondering aloud together, when we heard the Land Rover — no more than a vibration of the ground at first, then it came into camp and stopped. The men got out and came toward us, all smiles.

"We've found Bob's lions," they said, "the whole pride!"

V

Lions are not animals alone: they are symbols and totems
and legend; they have impressed themselves so deeply on
the human mind, if not its blood, it is as though the psyche
were emblazoned with their crest. When you look into the
eyes of a free lion and watch the grace of his long stride —
all that extra, unused energy flowing under the skin; when
you see the noble-looking calm of the mouth and nose, the
proud authority of the bearded chin — mysterious reminder
of the faces of classic and mythological heroes — you recognize to your marrow that you were born with that image
already in you.

It is not surprising. Until about two thousand years ago
lions still roamed the Balkan countries and Greece, while in
the Near East, where they were deified, they were to be

found as late as the middle of the nineteenth century. Aristotle and Pliny wrote about them. Fifteen, in marble, were set to guard the birthplace of Apollo while two lions sejant stand over the entrance to the palace of Mycenae. Thousands of years before that our ancestors painted or scratched lion images onto the walls of caves in the Pyrenees and the Dordogne. All through history there have been legends about them; in the earliest of these they were symbols of resurrection, when lion cubs, dead three days, were restored to life by their mother's breath. There was Androcles' grateful friend (and more, like him) and in the Middle Ages that mythological creature, the mantichore — offspring of a lioness who was unfaithful to her mate and had bred with a hyena.

In Africa I have read that there are natives who still believe in "werelions." They are convinced that there are men able to turn into a lion at will, eat people and go back into human form or that the spirit of the dead may enter a lion — particularly the spirit of a chieftain or hero, since lions are primarily symbols of power, majesty and courage.

"Simba" they call him. When they hunt him, or face a danger they equate with facing him, they put on a headdress of his fur, a necklace of his claws or teeth. A young Masai *moran,* or warrior, likes to prove his manhood by going out naked, with no more protection than a shield of buffalo hide, to kill a lion or at least to "blood" his spear.

Man is the lion's only enemy. As for the animals he hunts, these know to a fine tolerance the exact distance at which they lose the certainty of escaping a lion's charge and it is a fine thing to see antelopes and gazelles safely grazing or drinking quite near a lion, one of the herd always facing and

intently watching the common threat. If the lion crosses
that invisible boundary of safety every head lifts at once and
turns his way; everyone is frozen at attention.

In the heat of the day they are mostly asleep so that,
excited as we were that the pride had been found, there was
no use in returning till late afternoon; the sun was already
too hot, the lions would be lying up in the shade somewhere,
hidden away. The tranquil midday hours were as rich as
usual — particularly full, I remember, of bird voices. In the
bushes closest to where we sat there was a repeated, im-
pudent *Pst! Here* I am! and the dark flicker of little bulbuls
agitating the leaves. In a large old tree on the opposite bank
of the river, black-and-white-casqued hornbills, as bizarre
as if costumed for a circus, laughed like clowns as they
hopped among the branches. In the mating season the female would wall herself into a tree trunk for four and a
half months, her mate bringing her all her food in his absurd
beak and occasionally — no one knows why — the gift of
a flower. That day, too, we first heard the honey guide —
a bird who eats the pupae of bees yet is unable to get into
a hive without help. The mind reels at the evolutionary
process which gave the bird his call — an odd, wooden rattle — which, if followed from tree to tree, men and some
animals learned led to wild honey.

Between sounds the stillness was so complete it seemed
more a tremendous presence — a vacuity which constituted
another kind of fullness. Our ears have lost the knowledge
of such silence, and, with it, the fine perception of the sounds
that appear in it. Here each bird sound — even those of
minutely different varieties of one species — were as distinc-
tive as instruments of the orchestra; a musician must be be-

side himself on this continent of over two thousand bird voices where one group of warblers alone — the cisticola — is divided into forty species according to the sounds they make; whistling, siffling, croaking, zitting; wing-snapping, winding, wailing, churring; rattling, tinkling, piping, trilling — and one prima donna who is accredited simply with — singing.

When the sun was no longer straight overhead but the heat — as it always seemed to do — accumulated to its peak, we went off with our towels, soap and rifle to bathe in the rapids. The banks, here, were parched and bare but between them ran a beautiful stretch of fast water. Edging the stream, grasses flowered at their tops into Fourth-of-July star rockets; over long flat ledges the water slid in clear coils and braids, talking in a multitude of voices, falling at the bottom into a dance of foam and a jiggle of transparent domes bursting into air. We picked out our pools and flat rocks and put our clothes away on the bank. Having soaped ourselves we threw basins of water over our heads, at each other, sluiced ourselves all over; lay down in shallow, natural bathtubs where little waterfalls ran over our shoulders, stood up in the wind and let the air play over us, stretched out on the rocks to dry. The rocks under you and the sun overhead were solid with heat so that it was like lying between warm blankets; the water was very soft, light, cool with the night's cold. The bath was a ceremony — a worship of the elements and a celebration of the body.

But how terribly naked the white human body looks outdoors! How odd and vulnerable skin is compared to animal fur and hide! There is something rather unfinished about us at the same time that we have an appealing, sentient delicacy. Animals are uniformly perfect, their motions and gaits — however beautiful — prescribed and limited. Our lines and gestures are implicit with potentialities; we are packed with meanings which most of us scarcely reveal but which in the intensity and expressiveness of artists, and lovers, suggests another state of being altogether — almost a different species. Our imperfection is a promise as well as a flaw.

Lying there bathed in the deep physical delight of nothing between one's body and the natural world, we were startled by a sound like a small plane. Overhead, two vultures dove down the sky without a single flap of their wings, leveled off and went away over the river bank at such a speed they looked as if they must be powered by small motors. Their passing sent a shadow over us as vultures always do: *to whom are they going?* A few boulders downstream, Bob appeared and called; he thought by the time we got back to camp and had tea it would be late enough to set out for the lions.

The men had left them in the morning about a mile from the river, at the top of a long gentle rise from which the land fell away in all directions. When we neared the top, Bob looked carefully about and drove toward a single, twin-trunked acacia which rose like a fountain out of the deep grass. There, against the foot of the tree, a big lioness lay on watch, front paws stretched out before her — a lion couchant on a coat-of-arms — while for thirty or forty feet ahead of her the grass, exactly the color of her coat, was pressed down and woven through with lions.

We came up as close as we dared and shut off the motor: they were just beginning to wake up. Two lionesses lay

stretched out to their full eight- to nine-foot length asleep;
a fourth, at the far end of the group, sat up and looked about
through half-closed eyes while everywhere in between
sprawled young lions and cubs of different ages and sizes.
Waking up, they yawned, reached paws out toward one another, rolled gently over. The first two to get to their feet
stretched luxuriously then walked over to the end lioness,
who nuzzled them and greeted them with soft, caressing
little moans before settling down to lick them slowly and
lovingly all over. One of the sleeping lionesses awoke,
ambled over to the other one, woke her and they rubbed
their heads together and set to licking each other's necks,
heads and shoulders with the most voluptuous abandon.
Fifty feet away in the Land Rover — which they ignored as
if it were a rock or a tree — we were struggling to keep
quiet, fighting down longings to stretch like them, even to
embrace and purr.

Slowly the eastern sky clouded over and closed to slate;
against it, the lions, still in full sunlight, turned deep gold —
like illuminated headings on old manuscripts. As the sun
lowered, the grass materialized more and more of them, dis-
closing through a delicate screen a face, head on, and
smaller little faces — each wearing a different expression; a
paw here, a white belly there. The shapes grew more animated, rolled and twined and interlaced, thrust heads out to
look about, stretched and arched backs. Over against the tree
the guardian lioness yawned again and again, opening a mag-
nificently pale pink ribbed arch of mouth filled with enormous shiny teeth. From somewhere in the writhing, tumbling
mass two cubs no bigger than house cats emerged — reddish
and spotted, with outsize fuzzy ears. Both at once ap-

proached the lioness nearest to them and fell to sucking; she
may or may not have been their mother since lionesses will
feed one another's young. A cub who looked too big for
such things, having watched them a moment, went to the
lioness at the tree and raised his mouth to her teats. She
stood patiently till he had finished, then, going right up to
the tree, placed both front paws into the crotch of the split
trunk and sharpened her claws: from where we were, it
looked strangely like praying. The ritual finished, she sniffed
the air, looked carefully about, and with great deliberateness
headed out into the sea of grass. We looked where she was
looking: a single topi, or hartebeest, was slowly crossing the
foot of the field, on her side of a row of trees. Within seconds two more lionesses were out in the grass with her and
the three fanned out, bellies low, every muscle and hair and
nerve magnetized toward the topi. He must have sensed or
seen them for he stood frozen. The cubs were now alerted.
In some way the youngest ones were instructed to stay
where they were and instantly their heads went down, the
little leaves of their eyebrows drew together in disgusted
disappointment. All the others headed out into the field, the
large cubs following the three hunters at a little distance.
For the first time now we could count them: there were
twenty in the grass around us, and the single brown topi
there at the bottom of the field — a statue of life-and-death
attentiveness. It was like a perfectly balanced ballet in
which one didn't know which was more important — the
grouped chorus of hunters or the single sacrificial victim,
that lone figure waiting, head high, for death. The sky,
meanwhile, had turned gun-metal dark except where pink
thunderheads piled into mountains over a distant hill. On a

branch of the lion tree, a ring-necked dove all the while kept cooing its gentle complaint: "I *told* you not to go! I *told* you not to go. . . ."

The hunters took their time, advancing a little, waiting, creeping forward again, never letting the topi out of sight. At least so it seemed, yet at some moment that apparently doomed animal must have slipped away into the bush and drifted off downhill and out of sight for suddenly it was no longer there and all the tension immediately relaxed. In twos and threes the lions now started to return, loping back uphill behind us, passing the Land Rover on one side or the other: their little grunting communications, their swishing along in the dry grass were quite audible. We turned our heads, following them, and were galvanized by what we saw: *we* were now the ones they were surrounding! Coming alongside, the young lions, who showed much more interest in us than their mothers did, flopped down into the grass at the edge of the Land Rover's shadow and lay there, watching us with their calm golden eyes the color of grass but light-filled, like shallow gravelly pools with the sun in them. Then came a moment as indefinable as that in which the topi had escaped, when the whole situation felt in balance and — as long as we remained quiet and unmoving — safe. In the dark curve of sky over the blond slope, a rainbow appeared, then a second one outside it; the dove cooed and cooed; it was a scene in Paradise. The lions returned to their play, the two littlest ones standing up on their hind legs in the grass and boxing — knocking each other down and jumping on the fallen one. As quietly as possible we backed away — they barely noticed our going — and drove home, past herds of grazing wildebeest and zebra, little

flocks of Tommies, past two hyenas — also just waking for
the business of the night and sniffing the air — getting to our
camp just as the first drops of rain fell and we were swallowed up in a huge storm.

Dinner that night was in our outer tent to the drumming
of rain; it was one of the times Njorogi served us across an
acre of wet and blowy darkness without cooling a plate or
changing expression. We were all very exhilarated and at
the same time thoughtful; when Nat said that it would be
an *honor* to die feeding such creatures, no one laughed and
there was only token dissent.

Waking, sometime during the night, to the strange quiet
of rain stopping, and hearing the silence repeatedly shaken
by lions summoning one another, I thought of the paradoxes
of what we had seen and how many notions had been upset.
Lions, those "ravening and roaring" beasts of the Psalms, had
a tenderness exceeding that of most humans. Animals are
naturally affectionate with their young, but how explain the
two lionesses licking and licking each other? Or all those
sounds of endearment that the whole community exchanged?
Also, and this was the greatest mystery: though I am as
frightened and awed by those great flesh-eaters as the next
person, yet studying and identifying with them for that hour
and a half had soothed and allayed something in me, speak-
ing to some common ground between my mind and body,
between the lions and me. Through and through, inside and
out, I felt connected.

Myths and folk tales are full of strange symbolic animals
representing our primitive forces, our instinctive inner wisdom. Climb onto the magic little shaggy horse as Conn-Eda
did in the Celtic legend, follow his instructions — even to

killing and flaying him, and you will pass safely through fire and flood, the homely little horse will in the end be resurrected and changed into the handsomest and noblest friend. Believe in and be faithful to the Beast and it turns into a prince. However superior to the animals you may think you are (the legends appear to say), you need them, you owe them a lasting debt.

Those great free animals had been a kind of mirror, reflecting what we had in common and illustrating us to ourselves. Anthropologists push further and further back into Time whenever it was that we broke out of the natural matrix we shared with the animals — leaving them to their single consciousness, stepping out into the new dimension of our own. What a walk into space! Aeons ago as that birth must have been, more than we know we may still be gasping for air and be dazzled by what, really, is "out there," trying to see it clear. The lion, particularly the female, knows a great deal: she has to in order to hunt and kill enough to feed up to four cubs while slowly and systematically teaching them to do it for themselves — a process taking two full years — yet she doesn't know that she knows; she moves through her world unaware of that further dimension of thought by which we are able to observe ourselves, remember selectively, imagine and create. She didn't eat of the tree of the divided mind.

Civilization separates us constantly further — from the animals and from the unity we once shared. They live on in it, single, dignified, perfect, though where can they go, except, as we seem to be arranging for them, into extinction? Whereas we swing, struggling, between all the extremes in this new universe of opportunities. It was not envy of their perfectedness which the lions made me feel but, rather, a wave of fresh understanding for the "flawed confusion of human beings" — the messes and tragedies of our lives and the evil that we do — while the achievements of reason and art, the triumphs of love, had never seemed so marvelous. Neither evil nor good, unconfused by our divisions, how purely the lions mirrored the Creative Spirit at work in both of us! Watching them, all division was healed.

The chorus, roaring antiphonally out there in the dark, was being added to. Was it my imagination that the earth as well as the air shook to its sound? I wanted to thank them. They, and all the creatures around us, were acting out for us — not tragedy, as the Greeks did — but the eternal marvel of created life. They returned us to our first reality.

Bob now had to answer a whole new crop of questions; he remained a genius at not being trapped into making unqualified statements. When we walked in long grass where lions might be lying, what did we do if a head poked up? Veer off? He thought so; or better yet, keep walking so the lion didn't see we'd taken notice of him. Would he stay put, then? Not necessarily; he'd probably walk away but he might come toward you. *Then* what? You veered; or stood your ground and made angry shooing noises at him. We shook our heads. But he told us about seeing two little Masai boys about ten years old guarding some sheep and a lion coming almost up to them. Without the slightest hesitation they dashed straight for him with their sticks and shooed him off, then walked back to the herd as unconcerned as if the lion had been a hen.

But all this was over coffee and thick slices of Kimani's

bread toasted over the fire and we had gotten up as usual before daybreak, had tea, and hurried out to find our lions again.

We called first on a huge congregation of vultures and hyenas, all busy with a kill hidden from us by bushes, but since they were there it meant that the lions must have left; we turned and drove for the lion tree. A little short of it, on the same ridge, there were heads in the grass and we found our pride, finishing up the last of a wildebeest. The head and horns were left, with the pendant beard; the rib cage, empty as a ship not yet fully beamed; the propeller-bladed pelvis and, scattered here and there like discarded boots, the stripped legs. Two cubs were still absorbed in eating away at the head: each time they raised it up, the fleshless jaws opened as though in anguish, shutting again with a loud snap as they let it drop. It was macabre, repellent, fierce: I had to steady myself, watching, and then a flicker of memory lit a whole scene of a picnic years ago at which one of our sons was chewing away at the remains of a whole T-bone steak, and I remembered too the delight at the family dinner table over roasts of beef with red dish-gravy and being allowed to gnaw chicken bones in one's fingers. Lions fierce? Because their mothers killed for them instead of a bloody-aproned professional in a slaughterhouse? Did it skillfully, too, so that the wildebeest had probably only a few seconds of terror before its neck was broken (the smaller antelopes are seized by the throat and die at once). And never kill more than are needed to keep alive and sleek and shiny-coated. And with nothing left over that they could possibly eat, while what they *couldn't* eat fed hyenas and vultures and storks. Lions, fierce? I repeated it and had to brace myself against nausea not at the scene in the grass, now, but against tidal-wave images of *our* ferocity.

The lions were wandering off in twos and threes toward a little copse in a valley till eventually only one cub was left at the kill and, a little away from him, one big lioness. When he had finished, she stood up, ambled over and finished off the head, tearing off skin, sinking her creamy-gold teeth into flesh and sinew and gristle. Finally she let the head drop and walked off through the grass to join the rest of the pride; following her we found them getting ready to lie up for the day in their grove in the hollow — cubs and mothers all; if the male lions were around they had long ago been given the first taste of the kill — the "lion's share" — and gone off somewhere by themselves.

It was the last time we were to see our pride. The afternoon — like others to follow — became progressively still, oppressive, hazy with heat and smoke. Long before the evening thunderstorm the air held its breath, monsters seemed to lie in wait. Perhaps our intense watching had exhausted us or we had seen as much as we could absorb, but whatever the reason, we didn't bother to look for any animals at all after tea but drove straight to a great live-oak Margaret had noticed several days before at the edge of the plain. We had named it "Margaret's tree"; leaving the Land Rover nearby, we climbed up into its branches — each finding for himself a wide bough or sheltering niche in which to sit. For a long time we stayed up there among the leaves, while topis and Tommies grazed nearer and nearer and never lifted their heads, and a parade of zebras passed underneath on their way to water. And the next morning we broke camp and moved on.

VI

THE TALEK is a tributary of the Mara, which it joins near
the Tanganyika border. It is a very different river. The
Mara is opaque, indolent, somewhat ominous, the Talek little more than a creek — at most places only a few inches
deep and very clear. It runs over sand, around innumerable
bends; has beautiful great wild fig trees on its high banks, is
a paradise for birds. At our camps on the Mara the boubou
shrike sounded through the hours like a refrain; here the
emerald-spotted wood dove mourned all day in descending
chromatics and a long retard, grieving, as the natives say:
"My mother's dead, my father's dead, all my relatives are
dead and I'm alone, alone, alone." There were squawks
from touraco, flutings of golden orioles and the liquid,
throaty cascades of the robin chat — one of the great song-
birds of Africa. But the first sound we heard when we arrived was a delicate, deliberate tune so consciously whistled
that you were sure someone would walk up to you out of the
trees — someone human. It was the whistling of the wattle-

eyed flycatcher — subtle, with various intervals of great musicality like themes of the most sophisticated composer. A year was to pass before I learned from a musician who heard the song on a record, that it is a theme from Strauss's *Salome;* only the last note was missing.

It was always something of a miracle how soon after reaching a new campsite — the Land Rovers white (or yellow, or red) with dust, and the boys having taken the tents apart into their dozens of component poles and parts, packed them and the bedding and our entire kitchen away — they then set tables and chairs out under new trees in a new setting and served us a meal. Margaret and I looked dubiously at the deep grass around us in which nothing stood quite level and there were ferocious little biting ants: this was the place where Bob told us he had brought his very first clients — an eventful choice he reflected, smiling, for they had surprised a leopard a few feet from the tents and one tent had had to be evacuated in the middle of the night when it became a throughway for safari ants. Worst of all, they had met a cobra.

I suppose the commonest question asked of someone returning from Africa is: did you see many snakes? In the Coryndon Museum Snake Park we did; on safari, not one. Snakes are not only anxious not to be seen, but are marvelously quick and clever about hiding and getting away: if you *want* to find them, you have to try very hard. Surely there were snakes around us much of the time and out walking we took pains to look where we put our feet so as not to step on a puff adder: his lethargy makes him most dangerous. But the nearest I came to seeing a snake was here at the Talek, when as I approached the edge of the river bank, the deep grass ahead of me divided in a series of curves and swayed back together again. For a long moment I stood absolutely still until that "quicker breathing, and zero at the bone" had been dispelled. Margaret frightened herself quite badly reading a book on snakes which Bob kept in his book box. He told us stories about snakes and how he had been able to save a little snake-bitten Somali girl with his anti-venom kit, but it seemed to me that the whole subject really didn't bear thinking about; one had to rely on the snake's gift for getting away as much as he relies on his perfect poisons.

That first afternoon Bob and Amyas and I went for a bird walk up the bed of the river. We waded in and out of the stream, clambered up and down its steep banks, squelched in our wet sneakers across sand bars scattered with droppings and pitted with footprints — cloven and round, three-toed and five-toed, all crisscrossed with the neat lines of spurs left by birds. Although there was no breeze down here, we were also out of the worst heat, shaded by tall trees. High up in their crowns in the brilliant air, sunbirds darted back and forth, igniting, as they flew, into little gold and amethyst and iridescent green flames. Busily drawing nectar from the base of parasitic red and gold flowers which grow out of the trees' foliage, they seemed like tiny acolytes setting tree after tree on fire. Violet-backed starlings, the color of sun through a violet petal, flew in and out of bushes along the bank, always a little ahead of us as if wanting to keep us in view. Delicate tapping sounds led us to woodpeckers with zebra-striped heads, hanging upside down from a branch, and when we walked along the top of the river bank, in the open, little dun-colored waxbills blew out of the grass in front of our feet with a flash of bills the color of bright red sealing wax.

The colors of African birds are only faintly echoed by the most brilliant of our birds — by cardinal and tanager, buntings and hummingbirds. They are also of a fabulous, extreme elegance — as high-styled as if dressed by the most sensational Paris designer. The angle of crests and the long curling trains; the striped vests, shocking collars and dotted flanks are of breathtaking inventiveness and whimsy. And what bills! Hooked and curved, sickle-shaped and toothed, bright-colored and banded with contrasting color — designed for picking or cracking, piercing, or cleaning and scraping: the imagination seems infinite as does the cunning play of co-inventing the appropriate fruits and nuts, carcasses, fish and insects to keep the birds alive. How was it ever conceived? How do the genes order one scarlet feather exactly here, to make that dot, or in certain side feathers on the vulturine guinea fowl, command a feather to have stripes on one side and polka dots on the other side, of the same shaft?

In front of me in the stream bed, Bob walked as he always did with his gun held in his left hand, his right on the bird glasses hung around his neck, though mostly he spotted birds without them. He was a patient bird watcher; when, after careful locating — "You see that bush; go to the forked branch above it — got that? Now in a little, toward the trunk" — and before we had seen the bird it flew off, he did his best to follow it or find another of the same kind.

Curve after curve we wound upstream, splashing as little as possible, attentive to every movement and sound, so attentive that even with that gun just in front of me I had almost forgotten animals. Rounding a sharp bend, Bob stopped so short I almost walked into him.

I wouldn't have believed there could be as much expression in a whisper as got into his: "Jesus — a buffalo!"

Enormous, head down, he stood in the stream bed with us, fifty or sixty feet ahead and facing our way. Turning on our heels we walked off as quietly as possible, watching over our shoulders to see if he was following, glancing up at the bank above us. When we were fairly sure he wasn't coming, we slowed down and caught our breaths and Bob stood there upbraiding himself for forgetting to round the bend far on the outside. Come upon unexpectedly, buffalo are most dangerous for they are alert, have sharp senses and are very crafty; moreover, a buffalo alone, as this one was, is usually an old bull who is cantankerous as well. From the first one I saw at the Mara, I found them very alarming: their charcoal color, the heads helmeted with the great down-sweeping horns give them a broody, sinister look. There is something mysterious about their shyness combined with that malevolent expression, the bovine appearance of a creature so ponderous and ready to use such terrible weapons. Perhaps they remind us of the violence one feels in some very withdrawn people, the unpredictable force in the dark sides of our being. If he had charged us? I supposed we could have scrambled up the bank though buffalo are agile climbers; more probably Bob would have had to shoot him.

It was good to come around a last bend and find that familiar little huddle of our tents, there across a last stretch of grass: my legs were achingly tired and the evening chill was insinuating itself right through my thin shirt. Margaret and Nat were sitting together at the green slat table under the trees — that table which, when we weren't at meals, held a water bottle and glasses, the tin of Bob's tobacco and the bird and animal and flower guides which were the first things to be unpacked and the last to be removed; it was as much the center of our camp life as the round family table in Victorian living rooms. They looked very peaceful and at home there in the rough grass, Margaret with head bent over her sewing and Nat reading aloud to her from *Remembrance of Things Past*. It was the first time we had not all been on an excursion together and, seeing them, my heart swept out to them on a wave of delight. What a marvel: they, and Proust, here on the bank of a creek in Africa at sunset! On a stage of unthinkable vastness an instant of reality which all creation and all Time had combined to bring about was suddenly, brilliantly lit: it was one of those extraordinary moments when the veil is drawn aside and we see reality for what it is — scarcely able to bear the fragility of something so weighted with wonder. It was as quickly over as the sun's going; in another sense, it is inextinguishably there. Then there was the simple goodness of a basin of hot water in which to wash, the long unhurried drink together while the fire was built up and the stars came out in millions and the crickets began their evening song.

When I think of the Talek and the country we cruised through the next days, it is like looking at a series of scenes on a long old tapestry — the greens of tree crowns alternating with yellow grass in diminishing perspectives, all the colors softened and dimmed by midday haze and the smoke of distant fires; only in the slanting light of early morning and sunset was it entirely clear. In the faded foreground grass — on which there is a bloom as on green and gold plums — all along the wall of trees are giraffes: big ambling bulls with velvet sacks of genitals, like those of young men of the Renaissance whom Signorelli painted, and delicately stepping cows with their calves close beside them. They move in front of one another, shift positions, stop and stare out of their enormous eyes fringed with movie-actress eyelashes. Out from the coves of forest along the river more keep coming: counting them is as hard as counting their attendant birds who rise, flutter and resettle on their backs and necks; when I finally succeed, there are thirty, streaming uphill toward us in a long line, closer and closer till they fill the foreground where something startles them and off they go.

Giraffes, when they really get moving, are like two imperfectly co-ordinated animals, a neck and head floating along on top of a cantering body, the motion rippling along the reddish manes, and the black fly-whisk on the end of the tail describing wild slow circles — yet you cannot possibly laugh at their charming, haughty elegance. Even their bones look aristocratic as we discovered on finding a whole giraffe skeleton, chalk-white against the charred grass on which it lay — every bone in place and undisturbed. One could imagine the fire protecting it with a ring of flame from the hyenas gathered around, howling and wailing, eyes like pink coals, until it was too late, the bone too hard for them to chew up. An exact anatomical drawing it now seemed, more exaggeratedly strange even than the live creature, the huge master templet for an incredible design. No matter how many giraffes we saw, there was always a shock of disbelief at their appearance and when they had left, the same sense of unreality and regret. "Aaahh, Aaah," Nat would murmur on a descending curve of pity so that we were always happy for him when we found more.

Across the middle distance of the tapestry winds the track leading into Tanganyika and a little above it, almost hidden in the grass, a pair of honeymooning lions, discovered in the very early morning just as the sun rode free of the hills and tipped the grasses with gold. Having left the pride, left everything including hunting and eating for the five days during which they stay close beside each other and keep mating, these two looked almost ready for return. Their ribs stuck out; the lioness had moved away from her lord and lay low in the grass without ever raising her head. But he held his huge head high and proudly and the dawn wind blew the mane forward over his eyes so that he looked at once awe-inspiring and a little foolish — as if he wore fancy-dress or was a smiling lion carved on a medieval pillar.

Deep in a thicket farthest away from the river and up near the sky, stands a pair of little dik-dik, shyly staring out of huge mouse eyes ringed in white. They are among the smallest of the antelopes, only fourteen inches high at the shoulder; their delicate two-inch horns stand up perfectly straight, between them a little rounded tuft like the receiving set on a Martian in a cartoon. They too stay close together; of all their kind, they are the only monogamous ones.

Nearby is a glade full of impala, vaulting into the air with unlikely, exultant leaps or stretched out straight in impossible broad-jumps — more than a hundred does and fawns with one lordly buck at their head, wearing his great lyre of horns like a crown. "The biggest harem I've ever seen," Bob says as the buck stops herding some overindependent does to chase off a group of young suitors who have wandered out of the bush. Scared off by his head-down charge, they trot meekly away.

Like so many places in the highlands, this glade seems to belong more to the sky than to the slopes leading up to it — it holds you a little above the earth, in a more intense light, more airy air. Seen from it, the warp and woof of grass and trees rolls on and away without break to the end of the world under its accompaniment of clouds — all of equal size and flying at the same height — sweeping westward in long, even lines like banners of the earth's progress through space. It is a sight that enlarges you and also fills you with the greatest loneliness as though you had been returned to the time before man had yet come into being. Our physical closeness and contact inside the Land Rover, the sound of each other's voices in the oceanic silence were overwhelmingly precious, then, even though moments before we had argued crossly whether there was one buck or two in that herd of impala. And when Bob pointed out that there was a large Masai village at the edge of the forest down by the river and we rocked away downhill toward it by the most direct route, we were suddenly as gay as if on our way to a party.

It *was* a kind of party, too, and compared to the village on the Escarpment, this was a metropolis. There must have been twenty or thirty huts in it and more being built; the central kraal was crowded with people, and with cattle milling about and mooing, being edged toward the entrance by herdsmen and dogs: it was so early they were only now being driven out to graze. From the moment we got out of the car, we were greeted by waves of chattering interest and chiming "Jambos," outstretched hands, requests to come and meet this man's father (a fine, thoughtful-looking person), and see that woman's baby, though the building didn't stop for a moment. Women with babies in their laps sat stripping twigs from branches while others piled them into bundles; postholes were being thumped into the ground in circles marked out by little piles of dung; uprights were getting tied together with grass — only a few huts were finished enough to be covered with hides or plastered over. At all times we were in a crowd of people having the greatest variety of facial type and skin color, from lighter than American Indian red to the blackest Negro; and there was one young woman whose beauty belonged to no known race but almost to a different order of being as though she came from a slightly different world. Nearly six feet tall, with a queenly carriage and slow movements, she had a moon-round face of extraordinary serenity; everything about her was calm and gentle and full of dignity — she seemed a sort of earth or moon goddess. It was hard to guess her age — the shaved heads, adorned ears and bibs of beads are uniform from little girlhood to old age — but she might have been about eighteen. "She's *my* girl," said Bob, patting her shoulder and though he said it in English, everyone around them laughed and smiled.

I had a sudden vision of eighteen-year-olds at home — sitting at snack bars in their tight pants and sweaters, barely distinguishable from the boys at their sides; dancing in dark discothèques the latest version of what these people had danced for thousands of years, with curiously inward-looking expressions on their faces; or going to a "formal" wearing the make-up of a demimondaine which they have been applying since they were fourteen. Were they not all disguises, imitations, masks? Like the masks and costumes of a fancy-dress ball they seemed necessary in order to act natural, as though it were impossible to do so in any other way.

The people swarming around us were wearing almost identical ornaments and body cloths but their personalities and expressions were so individual that I shall always see separate faces clearly — particularly that of one man, smaller and more wiry than the others, who had the most astonishing eyes I ever saw in a human face. Their vitality was startling, they danced with so much life whether or not he smiled: full of intelligence, attentive and directed, they actually appeared to flicker as if from inner fire. Only one face out of many looked sullen, and to this man Amyas held out the gift of an empty film case. Like a solemn monkey he tried it in the loop of one ear where it didn't fit, then in two loops of the other where eventually it slid into place and he gave a sort of general, propitiating smile. He was the only hostile Masai we saw; he was also one of the least intelligent-looking.

Two days later we revisited the same village and were greeted like old friends and swept in through the gate on a wave of welcome. This time the pockets of my bush jacket were bulging with sweets wrapped in sparkling cellophane or foil which I began handing out to the children. At once I was surrounded by all the women and children in the village, my hands at the center of a constantly widening circle of their extended hands — small, pale-palmed, insistent. Mothers with babies in slings indicated that there were two of *them*, so that I began giving out candies by twos; one tiny child held out a delicate little monkey-hand beside its

mother's. A constant murmuring, sometimes shrill chorus
of "*Au, Au*" (give, give) enveloped me; it was almost uncomfortable and would have been so had they not when I
put two last sweets back into my pocket and patted it —
immediately desisted, smiled and wandered off.

In this part of the country finding these people who are
so in tune with the earth and whose villages belong to the
landscape like a bird's nest to a bush, is a little like finding

the indigenous birds and animals. There was always an element of surprise and luck in it: a quarter of a mile farther away and that thorn hedge would have melted into the background; a different angle of view from the top of the ridge or eyes less sharp than Bob's and we would never have known the people were there.

I am still not sure how we found the herdsmen some miles downstream of us, unless it was by the brown and white of a few of their sheep seen against a far backdrop of trees. Most of the very large flock were under the river bank in so closely crowded a mass it flowed in a rich brown-and-white mantle over the bare earth and down to the water's edge. Four or five figures stood on top of the bluff above and at our approach a little boy ran wildly toward them, cape flying, waving a spear twice his own height, its point flashing in the sun. The men just stood there waiting for us, Biblical figures in a way, yet even older than that — going back to the very first men to collect herds at all — their weapons and capes of the same coppery brown as the patterns of their animals. Dust and bleating rose into the still air, there was no other sound. A very little boy seated on the river bank turned his back to us and huddled inside a magnificent cape of skins which he pulled up around him until the bronze oval of his head barely showed. It was a moment of intense expectation — even more so than our first encounter on the Escarpment — the men unlike any we had yet seen and armed with bows and quivers full of arrows, spears and clubs, one with a sword hanging at his side. Their heads were not greased and ọchred like the young warriors' — they looked both more austere and more mature. These were the really hardy Masai we had heard about — the herdsmen who sleep out under the sky protected only by a temporary thorn fence, living together by themselves with their flocks and the few boys they train to be shepherds. They looked it. Real men, staunch and bold and with wonderful assured eyes, yet, as they quickly disclosed, with the typical Masai gaiety. How these people laugh! — heads thrown back, white teeth shining, deep belly-laughs — at themselves, at the little failures of understanding between us, at almost anything we do. A paunchy little puppy lay at the foot of one of the men, in his shade; when he moved away, leaving the puppy to squeak and waddle after him, I picked the animal up and laid him on the dusty foot in the new shaft of shade, and the shepherd laughed with delight. When Nat — always the clown in that hat which was getting daily more battered and whose flame-colored ribbon one of the shepherds longed to buy — offered the puppy *snuff*, they all guffawed, and in the general convivial mood were quite willing to sell him three of their beautiful arrows. Down on the shore, meanwhile, the two boys were busy gathering up the youngest newborn lambs and dipping them in the river — three to a trip, collected and held in the most casual manner by their bunched feet and returned, trembling and bleating, to their mothers. The water, here, was quite deep: in the little cove ringed by the animals it shone like a light blue eye.

Even so small a river as the Talek nourishes the life around it for miles. From anywhere in the surrounding dry country where it is still in sight, you can navigate by the winding rich green of the forest it sustains. Game paths converge toward every opening in the bank; families of baboons troop through the grass to get to it, infants clinging to their mothers' bellies or riding like tiny jockeys on their backs.

Birds eat from its trees and the pied kingfisher hovers over its surface, watching for fish like a diminutive black-and-white helicopter.

Sooner or later each day we gravitated to it ourselves for baths, for refreshment, for play — finding at one place deep pools in which we caught more than enough fish for one night's dinner, at another, a chaotic spread of flat rocks making tables and places to recline and platforms from which to jump the stream. On one of these rocks was gouged out a game of Bau — twenty-four round holes for holding pebbles, arranged in two parallel rows — a game so ancient no one knows when it began and which the Masai and many other tribes play still. Scarlet dragonflies stitched the air over the pools; in the sand we found a safari ants' superhighway with overpasses and tunnels and feeder highways along which heavy traffic streamed, passing at key places between closely ranked forces of soldier ants whose pincered forefeet arched overhead like crossed swords.

Happy and absorbed, we spent several hours there, surrounded by choices: what would be fun to do next — fish? Watch birds? Collect pebbles or bathe? Whatever we did do, it was punctuated with a cry of "Oh, look at this!" and someone running and jumping over the rocks, carefully holding a tree toad or a fantastic flower, or maybe a pebble of which one edge was very oddly chipped indeed — which, yes, might well be a little finger-tool someone made and used here one hundred, two hundred thousand years ago. And then whatever we *were* doing meandered like the river itself into something else, a different activity.

Or no activity at all — which was the way we spent the last evening. We knew that the next day would take us into a region of roads and road signs, national parks, other people in cars: better relish the last of this. Sitting still in one place, not to watch the sun go down or the stars come out — not in order to see anything particular but just to let go even of expectation, is to invite marvels. It is an art and an increasingly difficult one to practice. Lying on a beach in the sun isn't the same thing at all: your eyes are closed or you are hoping to tan, or you are busy resting — making a point of that — and only if you are making no point of anything and at the same time staying as alert as you know how, do wonderful things happen. As Lao-tzu said: the virtue of a pitcher is that it is empty.

We went down to the river bottom, and sat on some strange black rocks sculptured into beautiful Henry Moore masses, polished until they were blue with sky and like silk to touch. Beside us the river moved very gently over sand, wrinkling a little here and there like the folds of a scarf. Fig trees gripped the steep banks, reaching sixty, seventy feet into the bright air overhead; directly upstream at the end of a straight stretch stood one whose roots made a sort of pillared room beyond which the river swept around a curve.

At first there seemed to be no life at all — only the soft changes in the air around us: drifts of coolness, waves of warmth from the heated upland, wafts of fragrance; then a sand bar materialized a tail-flicking sandpiper, oblivious of our nearness, and in a bush two fire finches mated — dancing, pursuing, fluttering among the twigs. Gradually, as though we had been continually moving and had now entered a new space, the air became filled with song: robin chat melodies, whistling of flycatchers, murmuring of doves.

At the same time the light began to go and the trunks and branches of trees turned copper, then red, then violet; green pigeons perching in their leaves were slowly burnished gold and bronze and up in the depths of the sky clouds piled into glowing mountains. You could almost feel the earth revolving away from the sun and toward night, carrying us with it at this still, singing center. More and more birds flew in for a last drink, dipping into their own reflections, and upriver, at the foot of the biggest tree, a little bushbuck who must have been lying there the whole time with his front legs tucked under him, rose slowly to his knees, unfolded his long thin legs and walked delicately away.

It all seemed like a gentle promise and one knew it wasn't; that the long hours of darkness ahead would bring death to some, heightened alertness and fear to all. Fire, blankets, hot food suddenly became treasures beyond all price. Even at home in our brightly lit rooms the primitive creature in us faces extinction every evening as the earth goes dark, and is drawn at each year's ending into a frenzy of lighting and glorifying home, reassuring everyone we know that we do indeed care, filling empty arms with gifts.

Here, in camp, we had a fire every evening and off at a little distance the glow of the cook fire lit up the boys' faces and the undersides of branches over their heads. There were flashlights and even one electric lamp, connected to the car's generator, which gave general illumination around where we sat, yet there was always the same race each evening against the dark, followed by the untellable comfort of being together and close, sharing communication as well as food. Nat and Bob prolonged this the most; every evening after we had retired they still sat talking, their voices rumbling gently on to the play of firelight on the walls of our tent. After they had gone to bed, the boys might still be talking; many nights we fell asleep to the gentle liquid sound of Kikuyu which is so perfectly suited to African voices — voices which seem softer to me than any others I have heard. Perhaps the hugeness of the land, the nearness of the vast sky, makes one drop one's voice instinctively.

And then, at last, the night's silence which, when there was no wind, was so deep that a leaf falling on the canvas sounded like a heavy weight and a sleeper turning over in the next tent, like an earthquake. The small groans and snores of sleep were enough to make one listen for lions and every night at some hour — usually between one and three — I lay and listened for big animals, any crack or sigh or rumble making me hold my breath. No matter how firmly I reminded myself that the animals avoided us, feared us, had enough to eat, I remembered stories of their entering tents, chewing on guy ropes; I thought of the herd of elephants at the Mara. Then in spite of fears, great peace descended — the softness of the air, the fatigue of the day, the comfort of my bed became part of my quietly flowing blood and I was dreaming again. I was gone. Most often, now, I dreamed of the creatures we saw or else of my childhood — almost never of my usual life. Although the nights felt very, very long and as if dawn, and birds, were never going to come, I learned again to lie awake or to sleep, either one, without caring. It seemed to be a lesson one had to leave civilization in order to master.

The drive to Seronera next day was long and hard. A great deal of burned land; a tortuous road which ran mostly

through scrubby woodland and had few views: by the
fourth and fifth hour it seemed endless, the seat of a Land
Rover unbearable. There were two respites. At noon we
stopped at an attractive newly built lodge — wandering,
amazed, across a lawn where people were sitting around a
swimming pool in deck chairs. Inside, next to the dining
room (tables charmingly set with place mats and linen napkins folded into peaked hats), more people sat in armchairs
with drinks in their hands. The men wore Madras jackets;
some of the women wore heeled shoes and pretty flowered
dresses. I could scarcely believe them. Then Bob whispered
in my ear: "Remember that poem about the woman seen
from the train?

> "O fat white woman whom nobody loves,
> Why do you walk through the fields in gloves
> When the grass is as soft as the breast of doves
> And shivering-sweet to the touch?
> O why do you walk through the fields in gloves,
> Missing so much and so much?"

The second stop was at the Tanzanian border, where —
between frontiers — we ate our picnic of cheese and sardines
and beer and had our last river bath. Sand River at this
point runs between and over and around every kind of rock
and stepping-stone: makes pools and rapids, sandy beaches,
reedy coves. Cleopatra could have had no more luxurious
place to bathe: a rock pocketed with natural shelves to hold
soap and creams, eau de cologne and powder; a waterfall
tumbling into the curving bathtub whose sandy bottom
sparkled with glints of gold. Behind a curtain of drooping
branches I reveled a last time in the cool air and cool water,

the hot sun and warmed rocks — every sense in harmony with the surroundings.

We needed that interlude for we saw almost no animals or anything of interest in miles of scrubby brush and burn and the other car had two flat tires which obliged us to wait for them to catch up. At one of these waiting-points two entrancing dwarf mongooses poked eager and curious heads out of a termite mound beside the road and studied us with the roundest, brightest amber eyes, and once while driving, Bob sighted a strange small gazelle in the middle of a thicket — the oribi — a bigger and redder dik-dik with a black beauty-mark on each cheek. They and two newborn giraffes, umbilical cords still dangling from their bellies like black string, were the only creatures for seventy-five miles.

In the late afternoon we came first to some remains of buildings, and more numerous road signs and intersections; then to a game research station and finally to the complex of buildings around the lodge at Seronera. Women workers and wives of workers walked along the roadsides, their skirts and shawls glowing like garden flowers at sundown, carrying babies in slings on their backs, bundles on their heads. Their easy, barefoot grace and rich coloring belonged to this earth like its own fruit while the white people we saw around the lodge seemed unfitted, ungraceful, even uncouth. As quickly as possible we escaped across country to our campsite two miles away, under beautiful flat-topped acacias, just as the hills bordering the Serengeti began to turn rose and violet and the last embers faded into ashes.

We looked around unbelievingly: that was a road there beyond our tents and now a car came along it and in the distance electric lights were going on. Our campsite had a number assigned to it and there was even a sort of permanent outhouse at some distance back from where our tents were set; our own familiar toilet tent had not been put up. I walked out to the small gray building with its corrugated tin roof, opened the poorly fitting door and went in. Something down the hole of the seat — a mere brush stroke of sound or sight — caught my attention: yes, there it was again, and the second or third time around I saw it was a bat — a large one, with a twelve- or fifteen-inch wingspread. Shutting the door quickly behind me and rejoining the others seated around the table, I told Bob there was something I thought he ought to know, and drew him aside to impart my awful discovery. He broke into a delighted laugh. Yes, he knew! that was always a *wonderful* place for bats! And not only bats, he went on, with a look of fondling memories, "Those huts are *excellent* for spider, ant and hornet watching — they all have their nests in there." But the expression on my face was acting like a brake for he suddenly stopped. "If you'd rather, I'll have our own little tent put up," he said with concern. I was never more grateful.

When we went to bed that night, he made one of the only definite prohibitions of the entire trip: we were not under any conditions to go either to the outhouse or the toilet tent during the night. Lions, at Seronera, had become a problem. They were getting too accustomed to people; they played with tent ropes like cats with string; a few years before, a man asleep in an open A-tent was dragged out by the head and fatally mauled. The lions we saw the next two days, being watched by several carloads of people at once, lay beside the road like so many skins on a furrier's counter: they looked more tame than dangerous, they had little dignity. But we didn't care; we had seen our beautiful pride and lions were not what we had come here to find.

VII

WHEN NJOROGI SCRATCHED on our tent next morning, the full
moon still hung like a lamp in the acacia branches and only
a narrow stroke of hibiscus pink brushed the dark eastern
horizon: we were after leopards and wanted to be out hunting by daybreak. They are the shyest of animals, increasingly so as more women wear their coats, and many trav-
elers go home without having seen even one. Sometimes,
however, you may find one lying in the early morning sun
at the edge of the bush before he hides up for the day, or
in the branches of a tree where he may have dragged a kill
and stuffed it into a crotch, or running between bushes in
a rough little glade. Even when in plain sight leopards can

be so hard to see that Bob didn't leave the looking to us alone but had Ngugi drive in order to give the hunt his undivided attention.

We cruised that morning along smooth sandy roads, the air as it swept over us very cold, the great distances of the Serengeti plain melting away into sky; more than ever it felt like being at sea, and for those who stood in the opened hatch like standing on a ship in the wind.

Very slowly we followed one side of a donga — one of the many which radiate away from the river — till it petered out, tree after tree and finally bush by bush into the empty plain, and then returned along the other side to the river and tried the next line of trees. Hunting like that for one particular kind of animal tightens attention and stretches expectation almost to breaking; we hardly saw gazelles and monkeys and birds; we barely spoke. Ngugi, his crimson and fuchsia tie knotted around his throat, drove with utmost concentration and obedience to Bob's instructions. It was a kind of duet — the *Pole, Pole* (slow, slow), *Simama* (stop), *Kwenda* (go) answered by the changing sounds of the motor and the swing of the steering wheel which gave a little squeak as it turned. The rest of us carefully divided the looking between us into quadrants — left and right, ahead and to the sides. It is amazing what four untrained people can see in stumps and mats of thick foliage, in a hawk's nest, an anthill, a log — among us we must have sighted forty probable leopards but the only new thing we saw in two hours was a far-off cheetah, running still farther away, until we were on the way home, had given up hope and were nearing the lodge when Margaret broke out with *"There's something! There he is!* A leopard!"

He lay sprawled on a smooth dead tree trunk which curved over the narrow river, sunning himself — more impressive and regal and voluptuous than could be imagined of any animal. The pelt was so brilliant it seemed to shine from within, the spots night-black against the brushed gold, and there was so much of it — all those extra loose folds to take care of big kills, lying flung across the log — that it gave him a look of the most prodigal splendor. The tail, snowy underneath and dead black on top, waved continually at the tip like a weaving snake, as irresistibly in motion as consciousness itself, as if the leopard were thinking with it. One huge paw hung indolently over the edge of the tree trunk. He turned his head our way, the long white whiskers spreading out from his face in two thick fans, gave us an uneasy look and poured slowly head first off the log and down into some bushes.

In quite a different sense from what the lions had done, he left me feeling I had now seen one of the world's great — a feeling not unlike that which one has after an outstanding performance by a great actor or musician or dancer. It is as if you had come very close to the source of creative energy itself — had been brushed by its passing. The shock of excitement is partly surprise and partly recognition: so *that* is it! The earth is suddenly richer.

What a contrast to a lion he was! Lions are animals of the sun, leopards seem to be of the moon. Though both hunt by night, the lion has always been associated with myths of the sun; he is shining and radiant; his mane frames him like the sun's rays. The leopard's coat is like the dapple of firelight and dark on the forest floor, his eyes are the pale gold of the hunter's moon. The natives say that his spots mimic the footprints of all the animals of Africa. More secretive, more sensual-looking than the lion, he belongs, you feel, to the Orient, in an exotic garden. And this landscape in which we found him was rather like that — now that having seen him and that it was broad day, we really looked around.

Where the Mara and the Talek are rough and rolling grass country with riverine forest, Seronera is a flat and cultivated-looking park between river and plain, particularly beautiful for its trees. Along the banks of the river the yellow-barked acacia makes a delicate chartreuse screen broken here and there by a sausage tree, rough-barked and muscled as an old oak, hung with the two-foot pods which give it its name. But it was the flat-topped acacias over which we exclaimed aloud and which made us look up from the animals grazing underneath them to the branches above. Clean in outline as a wineglass, the ribs flare upward with such harmonious variations that approaching a tree, passing it, looking back, is like circling a perfectly conceived sculpture — never quite the same from any two points yet always in balance. The flat top is no more than a single layer of lace against the sky from which hang — on one side of the tree only, and like decorations from a Christmas tree — the round golden balls of the weaverbirds' nests; they are the perfect finishing touch to the trees' straight-stemmed, clean-branched austerity. They must love the earth at Seronera, for they grow forty, fifty feet tall there and gather into the circumference of their shade large herds of gazelles — Grant's and the endearing little "Tommies" with the up-slanting black-and-white stripe on their sides, the constantly flicking tails.

Here and there along the river are the greenest oases, thick with palms and luscious grass around a clear blue pool where one may surprise a pair of stylish brown-and-white Egyptian geese or a collection of anxious-faced, graceful little vervet monkeys, sitting on the sand, dipping their hands into the water for a drink. It is a painting by Rousseau. But it is the "gallery-forest" — the long lines of trees raying out into the plain — which the leopards love and where, the next morning, we found another — again after having searched fruitlessly for a couple of hours and almost given up. The tip of his tail betrayed him: a little higher than the tall grass and curled over like the handle of a cane, it swayed around in a hypnotic way, very black and white — unmistakable. This one was even shyer than the first had been, studying us for a long while from behind a screen of grass, then darting out and racing across the road right in front of the car — a muscled thrust of power, belly almost sweeping the dust.

As casual as the leopards were shy, a cheetah let us come to within ten or fifteen yards of where it lay reclining on a grassy mound like a voluptuous odalisque on a divan. It never did move away; when we had watched it as long as we cared to, we drove off. It has been said of the cheetah that it looks like a greyhound dressed in a leopard skin, which it does, except for a long black line leading from the corner of the eye to the chin — as though tears had left a black streak. If the lion is a royal animal, one feels that the cheetah belongs with royalty — perhaps because of the Assyrian bas reliefs where he stands beside the king for whom he hunted. Hooded like falcons, his ancestors were led out into the field and, when deer or gazelle were found, let loose to kill. With their great speed they don't need to stalk victims as lions and leopards do and, as though concious of this superiority, have the haughtiest arrogance to their stance, the lift of the small neat head — in strange contradiction to that touching line of tears which makes them look as uncertain, hungry and vulnerable as anything else that lives.

Seronera was rich with contrasts and extremes: fruitless hunting and last-minute luck; cold, limpid dawns and dreamlike sunsets of the most caressing beauty; oppressive middays made all but unbearable by tsetse flies, whose sting is so sharp it is hard not to shout when it drives in, and by a plague of bees. Anything in the least moist attracted them — they collected in washbasins, clustered on a facecloth hung up to dry, poured in swarms over the lips of pitchers. I covered and hid and shut things away inside netting; buttoned my shirt to the top, pulled down sleeves, tucked trouser legs inside two pairs of socks since the tsetse bit right through one, smeared exposed skin with preventatives, but when the wind dies, the insects bite, the birds fall silent, it is as if a malevolent spirit hovered over the land: you even begin to feel doomed and a little crazy; "they" — all the inimical forces of nature — are out to get you and the balance is all on the side of death. One day Margaret turned to me, her serene and distinguished look undone with contrition: "You know," she said, "I've been going around for years talking and writing and lecturing about the balance of nature and yet I don't think I ever really thought of myself as being involved in that balance — of being a *victim!*"

Here, even if no lion came into our tents, we were victims — of flies and heat, of getting trapped one afternoon in another of those purgatorial landscapes of rock and thorn from which every way out was barred — by a ditch, by the river, or otherwise impassable terrain and inside the hot, buzzing car we slapped and shoved at flies. Such misadventures are of one's own making; they are a part of the greater adventure and if one cannot take them it is better to stay home. What they did to us as a group was to silence us: there simply seemed nothing to say, no answer to be made. Bob, too, grew very quiet, refraining from any statement that smacked of excuse or apology although it would have been so easy to say "I remembered it as being over there" or "This is bad luck" — any of those "I thought's" and "I tried's" with which we attempt to gloss over trouble and soften others' possible criticism — he just worked at getting us out. And as with his refusal to reassure, one came to respect the natural and fatalistic wisdom of it: being sorry wouldn't get the flies out of the car or the car out of the ditch; being miserable and out of luck was as much part of a safari as being ecstatic and finding what you looked for.

We had good luck, too. Some distance out from Seronera at the edge of the Serengeti lies Lake Magadi — one of several lakes in East Africa of that name, which means Soda Lake. The chemistry of these bodies of water is exactly right for maintaining the algae and plankton on which flamingos feed, but since flamingos are the most mysterious of birds, one can never predict with any certainty when they will be on a particular lake or — if they are there — how long they will stay. "No flamingos," we had been told at the lodge; "they left over a month ago." But we had seen two leopards and were plagued by the tsetse so we took a chance and went anyway. Also, we had seen a giant eagle owl staring at us out of a fever-tree and Amyas, ever since a trip to Greece and rereading the *Odyssey*, was sure that owls announced the presence of the goddess Athene and meant good fortune.

A fair road took us south along the foot of a line of barren hills on our right, the plains reaching out to infinity on our left. But however barren and dry the African earth, the play of light upon it seems to make it glow with shifting colors as if it were opal, not dust, so that the hills unrolled past us in constantly, delicately changing splendor. At a hollow where water covered the road and we were about to ford it, thirty or forty fat little sand grouse flew in just in front of us, folded their wings and went in to drink; they might have flown thirty miles for those few swallows of water. We waited quietly and watched them till all at the same instant they lifted off the sand and wheeled away — then lumbered through the water ourselves, painfully thirsty at the splashing sound and at seeing the liquid sky under us stream with ripples.

Everything ahead and to both sides was stone dry. The heat was beginning to quiver along the surface of the plain, blurring its edges and colors, covering it with an element which wasn't air or fire or water, yet had the qualities of all three. It flowed, it flickered; even though you saw through it, it was thick and viscous-looking; the sight of it made the backs of your eyes feel hot, your throat dry.

We drove along the lower slope of the hills, the ground tilting toward the sun and that heat rising off the plain, around us the grass burnt to straw and no other vegetation in sight, when incredibly a tree appeared of the freshest, most vivid green. There was no other tree around; it was as perfectly shaped and rounded as some orange trees are, or the trees in medieval paintings of Paradise under whose boughs the blessed are greeting one another and embracing. Seen against the sere hillside its leaves held an unearthly vitality and seemed to move in a nonexistent breeze. We came nearer and saw that they *were* moving: they were

birds. The entire bare tree was thickly leafed with love-
birds, glossy green as the lining of a pod of June peas and
wearing on their heads a touch of orange bright as a coin of
sunlight in shade. Once on a February night, in a winter of
my own as well, I dreamt that the tree standing outside my
window was leafed all over with small brilliantly colored
birds all fluttering and twittering together. Bathed in that
unmistakable light of dreams which one recognizes at once
as important and not just the old junkyard of the day's dis-
cards, it was a deeply stirring sight and now here it was
again — in fact, shared with others, real. Real? The bird
tree of my dream carried with it such an aura of joy and
anticipation and so changed my outlook for days it must
have radiated out to those around me: didn't it have its own
order of reality?

The road wound and wound along the foothills until in a
shallow dip of land ahead we saw the lake shine up through
the quivering heat, its edges green-white with drying soda
and two or three of its coves clotted with pink as if solidly
carpeted with pink water lilies. A little nearer and the pink
took on more shape, became a pavement of round shells,
and now some detached themselves and flew up, unfolding
flashes of cardinal red with sharp black edges, swooped and
circled and came in for a landing, thrusting long slender
legs out to feel for the water, treading it rapidly till they
came to a stop and settled back into the flock. Not only were
there flamingos, there were thousands upon thousands of
them.

We drove slowly down toward the shore to a place where
the car would be partially hidden by thorn bushes and tall
grass. At our coming, a spotted gold shape, waving a black
and white tail, slid away into a thicket — and this time we

hadn't even been looking! When the motor was turned off, the air filled with a great susurration of massed sound, like the responses of a congregation in a vast church, rising now and again in a crescendo till it became the sound of an angry crowd. In the nearest cove the flamingos were jammed so close it was a wonder they could move at all; if one raised its head hundreds went up, if one flew, so did all its immediate neighbors. The nearer, more detached ones were walking slowly about eating, heads upside down in the water to the eyes, sieving plankton and algae out of the water they took in and strained from their bills. A few greater flamingo, the kind who may stand six feet tall, were doing a dance, treading rhythmically in a full circle around a central point, trampling the soft bottom to raise more food. Farther out from shore more greater flamingo — twice as big as the lesser birds — stood sleeping, necks curled into elaborate loops and knots, the head ends tucked under on their backs. Across a farther stretch of water still, a long line of birds coasted along, each swimming at exactly the same speed and all with their heads in the water, giving them a strange trancelike appearance, as though they were performing a mass meditation.

Having watched them for a long while from the car and in a kind of trance ourselves, we got out before leaving and walked down to the shore. It was a curious crust of soda, sand and droppings lapped by the thick green lake water — an algae soup fertilized by the birds themselves. The water was soft and slippery and smooth to touch; little unfolding waves added their small sound to the greater pervasive murmur. Feathers lay here and there on the sand or rocked in the scum and I began collecting them and putting them in

the pockets of my bush jacket — white ones with the faintest
flush of pink, coral, deep rose. From here the enormous
numbers and hypnotic movements and sounds of the birds,
the variations of color — like masses of roses — made them
seem less flocks of birds than a ballet, a movement of cloud,
a kind of music.

It was hard leaving; we kept putting it off — taking one
more picture, picking flowers, watching just one more take-
off, another landing. It was beautiful and unearthly, that
concert of color and motion — a hundred birds turning in
flight making petal after petal of color unfold, a flock becoming a single, blowing veil. The wonderful synchronous flights
of birds in the fall — those unwinding ribbons of starlings

and wavering V's of wild geese — are far overhead and quickly gone; the group actions of bees and ants are difficult to follow, but this was at a scale and distance one could comprehend. What a "participation mystique"! Community, to these birds, is everything; they are the only known creatures who, if necessary, will choose the group ahead of their own young — abandoning unhatched eggs or young birds too small to fly if the flock decides to move. No one knows all about them or fully understands them.

Leaving Seronera the next morning was not hard; we had seen what we came for and were ready to push on to the crater of Ngorongoro whose outline we had kept seeing dimly at our farthest points of leopard hunting. Preparing for that day's drive was like getting ready for a rough day at sea only it was dust that had to be kept out, the bone-dry Serengeti we were to cross. In order for the two cars to travel together we waited at an oasis at the edge of the plain

for the boys to catch up with us, happy to savor the delicious sweet air of early morning, the sunlight which at this hour was a blessing. The gray-eyed goddess must still have been with us for there in the grass beside the track lay a fine male lion. For a few seconds he looked directly at us, chin lifted, amber eyes half closed, then his attention abruptly shifted and focused on another big male walking toward him through the trees. When only ten feet or so of sparkling grass divided them, the nearer lion stood up, advanced and the two greeted one another — rubbed their huge shaggy heads affectionately against one another, over and over, uttering little moaning grunts of endearment like those we had heard between the mothers and cubs of our big pride. With a last placing together of their wide foreheads, they separated and looked about consideringly, then walked off, side by side, into the rising sun. The tenderness of their meeting and the radiance of the newly created day brought us into that blissful sense of harmony which more and more we were discovering was Africa's gift. The walls inside you, and those between you and the world, dissolved and disappeared; whatever it is that divides ceased to exist; it had never been real in the first place, you felt — it was some kind of conjuror's trick. One felt sustained by, and sustaining, a live, fluid matrix as pervading and boundless and unfamiliar as love.

Once out on the plain, beyond the last tree, the last bush, we were at sea, on a burnt, lifeless-looking surface that soon shimmered with waves of heat. Finally even the *kopjes* stopped — those strange outcroppings of oddly shaped boulders and rocky towers which look man-made, as if they were abandoned castles or fortified towns. Like a chain of islands they petered out and dwindled away astern till everything in sight was level except the far blue outline of mountains, fainter than cloud. Ahead, the road ran straight to the horizon where it seemed to fall off the edge of the world. Sometimes a car came from there, appearing first as a whirl of dust, growing a dark seed at its center which swelled in size until the car was upon us and we quickly shut even the small ventilators which were the only apertures left open; inside the car, even with everything closed, we sat in drifts of dust settling on seats, clothes, getting into eyes and nostrils, sifting like blown snow over every surface. As the heat grew, mirages appeared all around us. Land turned to sheets of water; the sky lay in huge lakes beyond which stretched a farther shore or else the plain suddenly stopped and there was the sea — the sea! — winking and shining right off into space with no discernible line between. Here and there dust whirled up into inverted cones or columns that spun — wildly gyrating — across the surface of the earth and out of sight. Some trailed diaphanous appendages — dancers unwinding themselves from veils; others grew at their tops heads and arms and waving fingers, hovered like jinn, then collapsed and vanished — *fft!* It seemed impossible such a devil's playground was ever green and flowery and flowing with thousands of animals; certainly nothing could inhabit it now — and yet it did: there were ostriches standing high as a man or hunting in the dry grass for lizards and crickets; there were sandgrouse and fat little francolins and crowned lapwings whose babies are so perfectly camouflaged that even when they are pointed out, you only see them because they move and the grass stands still.

It is hard to think of ostriches as birds at all when, in their way, they are as unlikely as giraffes. Though the females are uniformly dun-colored and dull, the male has a queer elegance and, when he is courting, great grace. He does, then, a rhythmic dance in which he sweeps first one wing and then the other over and across his back in beautiful fanlike sweeps. When this is performed by the sharply black-and-white ostrich who lives in the north frontier country, it is an unforgettable sight. All ostriches have naked legs, fattening at the top like a woman's thighs and when the excited male's legs turn a deep pink (or as with the northern ostrich, an intense turquoise) under the thick soft skirts of down, the resemblance to human can-can dancers is ridiculous and obscene. But there were no courting scenes out on the plain — only searching for food and wildly weaving running away.

At last a hill appeared — a real one which the road climbed over and down — and after a few miles more of plain, there was first one lone tree, later a thin line of them, finally a donga and, crossing the land ahead, the green borders of Olduvai Gorge. But the devil saves his best trick for the end: just before the gorge where there is the first promise of green, rise weird sand dunes which move slowly as glaciers across the land with the wind. Wrapped by the steady stream of air into a smooth crescent, the dark gray powder is piled forty or fifty feet high, its top forever blowing and sliding off a knife-edge like snow from a cornice. We got out and climbed a dune — ran all over it and jumped in it, kicked sand off the edge which poured down the slope in dark streams like a fluid. On the windward slope lay a little mottled dragon of a lizard who, when we came close, rose up on his legs and puffed himself threateningly out. We wondered what there was for him to eat in his curious moon-landscape until we discovered masses of dead beetles about; wind blows them into the dune where the powdery dust gives them no traction for taking off again: they starve to death and the lizard lives.

Olduvai Gorge — a crack in the earth's surface about half a mile across and no more than three hundred feet deep — is a kind of little Grand Canyon of animal and human remains. But it is small in spatial dimensions only, for the meaning and implications of what it contains are too big for our brains to comprehend. A combination of geographical, geological, and evolutionary events have made it the repository of enormous numbers of creatures who lived there across the last two million years and maybe even more, including the earliest near-humans (hominids) yet found. What is now thought to be the cradle of our race is as full of bones and fragments as pudding stone is of pebbles; one can scarcely take a step there without coming on something out of the past and a cut into the bank may expose the bones of a number of long extinct animals — giant pigs with tusks twice the size of an elephant's, giraffes twice as big as ours, or the bones and tools of our very earliest ancestors. The gifted and energetic Louis and Mary Leakey, with their three sons, have made the most remarkable finds and have there a laboratory and camp, but on going to call, we found they were in Nairobi.

An African guide took us to see the chief sites. From his hut on the rim, we drove down through stratifications of different colored rock and clay to the floor of the canyon, up the other side and along its top, down again. The bottom at midday was a barbecue pit, and walking on the whitish gravelly rubble like wading in bones. A lake once lay where we were; an earthquake or volcanic disaster of some sort filled it in and buried everything; another upheaval which rent Africa from one end to the other, leaving the six thousand miles of crack known as the Rift, split it open again: across periods of time too big to grasp, these remains around us were alternately buried and unburied, heaped on top of one another, rocked together and shaken apart.

We came to a little roofed-over place and standing gratefully in the shade heard the guide tell us in his careful, soft English — it sounded like a foreign language — that this was the site of what was presumed to be the earliest human shelter. From under another little roof he began picking things up off the whitish gravel at his feet, where numbered labels indicated where they belonged, and brought them to us to examine. There was a clump of huge teeth whose enamel still had a glossy vitreous polish: these were the molars, he explained, of Dinotherium, an elephant whose kind died out three hundred thousand years ago. There were round stones just right to hold in the hand which had been shaped into axes, and little pieces of flint with one edge chipped sharp enough to scrape flesh from a hide — tools that could be held between forefinger and thumb. On the other side of the path from us a rough circle of stones outlined the shelter in which these first toolmakers had protected themselves from the sun and the rain.

Dazed with heat and with the meaning of what we were seeing, we handed the treasures around to each other and back to the guide who gently replaced them on their dry bed. Down there in the bottom of the gorge, at its lowest, earliest level of Time, nothing moved or made a sound but ourselves, and our voices dropped almost to whispers. No church, certainly no museum, could feel as this place did: to pass one's fingers over the still glassy enamel of a pre-elephant's teeth and hold in the palm of one's hand an object painstakingly shaped by some ancestor who tramped about here unthinkable ages before, is to feel one's own selfness, and solitude, melt into the tremendous stream in which we are all immersed — to become strangely reconciled, too, to one's own part in it, brief and microscopic and intensely personal as that is. What began as awe softens into comfort. Passing time evaporates like moisture in that dazzling air, for almost two million years later we are still part of that same continuous procession as were these experimental forms of life that preceded us. They contributed to what now is, as we contribute to the unimaginable future. Nothing, nothing at all is wasted! This dry silent valley of bones shines with a peace as palpable as its throbbing heat.

Driving, that afternoon, up the pass to the rim of the crater, we left all sense of time and even of the earth behind; it was like climbing a road in the sky. For an hour, perhaps, the edges of Olduvai still drew a wavering green across the plain, then it, too, was lost in the panorama which, though it filled half the space at our backs, grew as faint as if painted on gauze. In the morning the same view would be so clear you would be able to see the kopjes at Seronera sixty miles away — each morning in Africa the world is created again — but as the sun climbs and the heat rises, everything dissolves once more into haze as if it had never been.

Each time we thought we had come to the rim, a curve led to another loop of bone-rattling washboard road. The engine labored; the air grew so cold we put on sweaters, then jackets and scarves. To Bob's "I think that's it right ahead," we no longer made even token replies. When finally we were standing in the wind in that break of the ridge which gives the first view into the crater, we were as unprepared for it as if we had never seen pictures of it or known what it was. How can the eye measure, almost two thousand feet below, a circular world of plains dotted with animals, an expanse of celadon-green lake, forests, hills? Twelve miles away at the opposite rim it comes to an end: very near for the edge of a world, for the other side of a crater unthinkably far. All proportion is lost. Looking back, now, we could see nothing but sky, the slope on which we stood, the empty road. The air quivered with light, the sun felt very close and blazing hot; we stood in the wind and shivered.

Around a few more curves of road, the barren upland turned into cloud-forest and we were in another world still: a giant's garden which clouds drifting and hanging over the rim keep moist and green. We got out and walked into groves of trees bearded with moon-green moss and hung with vines, down long aisles which ended in air yet looked as though they led to formal parterres and pillared mansions. All around us flowers stood higher than our heads: acres of orange leonotis growing in a series of wheels up stalks seven feet high; even higher, clusters of a fragrant white flower like the bouvardia in brides' bouquets; deep rose hollyhocks; a purple-blue ageratum six feet in the air. Weaving in and out among the blooms flashed quantities of sunbirds — if you missed seeing one, another would dart into view so that our cries of "Oh, look, look at *that* one!" "Where?" "Oh, he's gone" had refrains of "Here, that flower," and "There's another, and another!" We pushed on through the towering blooms in a warm reek of broken stems, peered through the trees to where the land fell away, following the gleam of birds who in full sunlight were each a blaze of iridescence or metallic sheen: golden-winged with long black tails or wearing double collars of two colors, one — the malachite — a solid intense green like the flame from copper in a driftwood fire. And on the branch of a tree I found one of their nests: a delicate little hanging basket carefully embroidered on the outside with lichens, sequinned with the wings of insects which glittered softly as the breeze swayed it.

Then down the precipitous road to the crater floor — like going down the inside of a bowl, the road, steep as a flight of stairs, cut out of the side of the hill and only maneuverable by four-wheel drive in low gear — to our camp. It was already set up — under a fig tree so ancient, so huge it sheltered all our tents, the kitchen, the table and chairs. "We're the only people except Masai living down here," Bob told us and pointed, with his arm at more than 45 degrees, to the tourist lodge, all but hidden in cloud on the rim above. "It's quite nice up there actually; you have a fire in your room in the morning — lots of comforts." But this was after we had taken a walk onto a little hill and the men had gone for wood and built up *our* fire and we were at home and together, at peace and warm.

Had that all been one day? The sunrise greeted by lions and the desert which took all morning? Noon at Olduvai held the entire Age — long or short — of Man; in that wonderland up on the rim we had returned to our childhood and now we sat around a fire on a volcano's ancient floor, the sunset clouds drifting over us like flamingo feathers, settling softly into night.

VIII

It began with a succession of sharp dry clackings, rather like fearful burps or a terribly sticky door being forced open by degrees. Then it climbed into a series of dying screams — piercing, huge in volume, gradually diminishing and subsiding. All of it seemed to be in the air directly over the tent, was as loud as a train whistle and so horrifying it was funny. After the first transfixed moments, we broke out laughing — or perhaps it would be more accurate to say into wobbly giggles. When nothing further occurred — no running footsteps or shots, no other animal sounds except a couple of repetitions from the banshee itself — we went back to sleep. Later in the night we were awakened again, this time by a monstrous crash, a long-drawn-out rattle of tin cans and a prolonged swoosh as of dragging skirts. I sat straight up in bed, shivering with cold, asking the dark out loud what *that* was, then, on hearing shooing-away shouts from the boys, it dawned on us that hyenas must have raided the food supplies. This time it was not so easy to go back to sleep, for the boys proceeded to talk in low, excited tones for half an hour or more without stopping, even though it was not yet five o'clock and of course blind dark.

Often I wondered how they felt about this whole business of working for people bent on getting as near to dangerous animals as possible, driving their belongings and housekeeping necessities across deserts and down precipitous roads, setting up tents somewhere between the droppings of elephants and the jaws of crocodiles. Njorogi's little sphinx face revealed nothing. Kimani, with his gentle *Ndeo's* and *M'sabu's*, was the height of courtesy and Ngugi looked calm and patient enough whether at the wheel of a Land Rover or toting heavy tins of water up from a river. Mightn't they all the same just get fed up some fine day? Or, more likely, some dark night when silence was ripped open as this one had been? I brooded quite a while on the probabilities of their quietly taking off in the other Land Rover and how Bob would handle *that*.

But Bob had heard nothing at all. When we forgathered for breakfast, wearing woolen caps and mufflers and ski sweaters against the cold which a heavy layer of clouds held down overhead, a line from his pillow still creased one cheek and he had slept wonderfully, he said. The noise? That would be a tree hyrax; it probably lived in the fig tree over our heads. Hyenas take food? He called out to Njorogi who came to him with a long and gentle tale, later given the most cheerful additions by Kimani and Ngugi; it was quite apparent no one was leaving in a huff for Nairobi. But after breakfast we all set about searching for lost articles, fanning out through the waist-high weeds between camp and the grassland. There we found the tarpaulin used to cover the food supplies, an assortment of cans — two punctured as if by a beer-can opener — and a long trail of flour leading to a torn bag. Two nights later we were to be raided again, the soap powder and beer sampled, and a kerosense tin disappeared which we never did recover.

Later that morning Amyas was studying our great tree trunk's multiple archings and flutings, as complex as those of the pillars of York Cathedral, when he noticed that he was being watched from inside a hole by a dumpy little being with very shiny eyes. It was our hyrax all right, but how could that engaging figure straight out of Beatrix Potter, or *The Wind in the Willows,* and no bigger than a woodchuck, make that nerve-splitting sound? They are shy nocturnal animals, yet when we gathered around he peered out at us and studied us with the most intense interest. He's a naturalist, said Bob.

Wildebeest, meanwhile, were slowly covering the slopes above camp, and groups of zebras wandered near, looking less concerned about us than any others we had seen. One expects zebras to be much less wild than they are; they are so near being horses, there is something so comfortable and domestic-looking about their friendly, decorative faces, their fat rear ends with the tails which appear to be braided at the root; yet they startle surprisingly easily and just when you think that this time you are going to get really close, away they go, striping the wind.

In the crater, just the same, we came closer to animals, or were more aware of them being around us than we had yet been. Some of this was visual — in that great open bowl they were nearly always in sight — but, even more, they were actually contained here as they were not in any other landscape. There is a little traffic back and forth over the rim but the crater is mostly a stable and independent world supporting almost every kind of animal except giraffes and crocodiles with its pasturage and forest, streams and swamps and with plenty of game to feed its predators.

Very soon the eye, as well as some subtler organ of perception, defines and accepts the crater's limits, but it takes longer to learn its inner dimensions and proportions. Looking across a marsh at the crater wall you see some small dark objects which appear to be birds just beyond the reeds, only to realize that they are wildebeest miles away. A low hill rises against the backdrop of cloud forest — massed with the vertical stripes of tall tree trunks and hanging vines or else patterned with the dizzying horizontals of huge acacias — but when you drive up it, the hill turns out to be a small mountain and there is still a valley four miles across between you and the steep rise ahead. In the days we were there these effects were heightened by an almost constant cover of cloud, still further enclosing us. Occasionally long beams of light broke through, and then stage spots, focused from immeasurable heights, circled a far patch of grass covered with antlike herds, or lighted in a nearby swamp the blue eye of a pool.

The sense of emptiness and remoteness was overwhelming; such vacuity is almost a new element and whatever world once existed on the other side of that dim encircling wall becomes so ghostly it loses all reality to the mind. As on islands, the very limits which in time grow restricting are at first a great inducement to explore. Also, with the weather like late November at home, once the campfire was allowed to go out there was nowhere to keep warm except in bed, a Himalayan sleeping bag tucked around you. We went everywhere we could. We drove; we walked; we explored the shore of the soda lake where the ground was powdered white as if after a light fall of snow and the lake waves, like the beards of wildebeest drinking from its margin, streamed in the cold wind.

Once, in the Land Rover, we came upon an eerie scene of a kill, or a death. Several Masai women were walking away from it, carrying rolled skins filled with ribs and steaks and chunks of fresh pink meat. Where the cow had died every kind of vulture was gathered on the little that was left — the head, hooves, excrement. Squabbling and squawking, the birds were tearing at these while the Marabou storks, who can't tear the meat off but can only eat leftovers, waited quietly with their bills on their chests along with several smaller, less aggressive vultures. The biggest, fiercest-looking lappet-faced vultures had taken command, and were chasing intruders away — stalking in Prussian goose-step toward them, the big capes of their wings spread out menacingly. The air was filled with the noise of gluttony, flapping, threats. Those birds who were on the head were ripping the insides of it out through the eye sockets: bracing, they pulled at sinews and the meninges of brain, tearing and gobbling when these came free. It was horrible, macabre and fascinating to watch, yet when one thought about it, not ferocious at all — just using as food whatever has died, leaving the earth clean and fresh. Except for that giraffe skeleton at the Talek we had seen almost no bones in all the country we had come through, and perhaps a total of six or seven skulls with the horns still attached. The hyenas' faeces, white with lime, tell where the bones have gone; droppings which one sees everywhere, fresh, wash down into the earth and the streams; the leavings feed birds. Nothing, anywhere, is wasted.

Nevertheless it was beautiful to find beyond that scene a fresh, reed-bordered pool — a calm reflection of the clearing sky — in which more than twelve kinds of water birds were wading, standing, fishing among the green spears of grass. And in the grass above the pool, a group of crowned cranes walked about in stately grace, trailing their little crested coronets of fringed gold, the silvery-blue, slinky breast feathers looking like long-haired fur, a flounce of ivory where their white sides meet brown tail. Nothing could look more elegant, delicate, aristocratic.

Gradually, on circling the enormous cloud-ceilinged bowl and climbing up and down the foothills between lake and wall, we got a sense of its geography. That dotted line of bushes, those creases in the blond grass slope, marked the bed of a stream — all around the crater small clear streams pour down its walls to empty into pools and inlets and marsh and finally into the lake itself. Near to, with their banks of blowing wild flowers and voluble little waterfalls, they might be Alpine brooks in Switzerland. Fording one near our camp, we came on two naked Masai men standing in the cold dark water, washing themselves. Their wet bodies shone with the same gloss you see on the coats of topi; they gave us as natural a look.

But the black-maned lions for which the crater is famous we never saw, even though we hunted for two days in a row and for hours on end in the highland above a Masai village where we were told they had been seen. Two Masai friends of Bob's went with us as guides; sitting hunched up in the back of the Land Rover where our luggage was packed on long journeys, they peered excitedly through the dusty windows, pointing out different animals, giving us gleaming smiles whenever we looked around. Except with children I don't believe I have ever felt a more delightful and direct exchange than took place between us in that small space. We were unable to say more to one another than *Jambo, Kwaheri* (goodbye) and *Asante* (thank you), yet there was a quick and ready flow of gaiety, interest and goodwill. My light complexion and wind-blown nearly white hair seemed to please them as much as their greased and reddened caps of curls and the decorated loops of their ears fascinated me. It reminded me of seeing once in the West Indies some little black children arriving for a birthday party at the entrance to a white child's house and, before going inside, tenderly and delightedly fingering the pale floss of their small hostess's hair — so opposite to their own. I felt deeply ashamed that I could still harbor any reservations and disliked myself for it. I wondered if curiosity about and pleasure in people very different from ourselves isn't far more natural to us than the hostile suspicion we acquire.

The morning we left the crater, I went out for a walk by myself. It was the first time I had done so and I took care to stay well away from clumps of bushes and from a sandy

track which was heavily rosetted with the spoor of lions.
Although I was out of sight of camp it was easy to tell where
it lay from a slash of burn in the grassland above it and from
the green dome of our cathedral tree, dwarfing every other
tree in the vicinity.

If walking puts you into closer connection with your surroundings than cruising in a car, walking alone is as great a
step further still into feeling the unity in which you belong.
When the last faint vibration of the human voice is lost and
you first enter the enormous stillness, it is disquieting, it
makes you overconscious of yourself but soon it welcomes
you and you are taken into it as into a new element; you
begin to hear and see and smell as if those senses, before,
had been muffled and fogged and vitiated. Then comes an

extraordinary fresh awareness of yourself as a human being
among other beings.

My hope was to get as close as possible to the zebras and
wildebeest, the jackals and baboons which were all around
the area between our camp and the deep forest of fever trees
where, day and night, elephants could be heard at their
noisy browsing. I also wanted to find again if I could, and
see close to, a group of eland the Land Rover had frightened
away — noble, archaic-looking creatures and one of the biggest of the antelopes. Up to a point I succeeded but with
every encounter the same thing happened: as soon as I came
within what seemed a certain magic distance of the creatures, no matter how quietly and gently I moved, they
drifted away — politely, unhurried, and sometimes with a

look over a shoulder that seemed to be saying "If you don't mind, I've got to be going along now," but always away. A baby zebra, still hazed over with a chestnut-brown fuzz, hung back longer than the rest of his herd, then something happened inside him too, and with a little forward plunge like a pushed rocking horse, he bounded after them. When I saw a jackal in deep grass, very carefully stalking and pouncing on crickets, I was sure his concentration would let me get near, but at about the same critical distance he looked up from his hunting, studied me and trotted off.

This proof of being the one creature all others fear and leave alone (unless cornered or surprised with young, when, even then, their charge may be only a token charge, a warning) is very disconcerting. All that giving way makes you feel so important and lonely — the way royalty must often feel; it is like being the negative pole of a magnet, surrounded by a powerful, invisible field of force. But then comes the realization that zebra and jackal, and the great eland, do not know themselves. It is we who do that for them, who are able to confer this honor upon them and who can allow them their beautiful dignity.

Leaving the crater seemed a total unreality; remote as on some other planet, how could one believe there still was a world, that anything existed beyond the rim in its wreath of cloud? With the Land Rover barely able to hold the grade, we climbed up through mist and towering cloud forest, eerie with tall trees wearing their foliage only at the very top, past swinging vines and serpentine branches, past prehistoric-looking wide-leafed plants. Up the winding, steep road three different Masai were slowly toiling — two women, one of them pregnant, and a man alone who stopped at the same little waterfall we did where he carefully washed and scrubbed his feet and legs using a stone for soap. Along the crater's rim we saw nothing at all but the ghostly silhouettes of trees and, in the nearby road bank, as if under a magnifying glass, masses of wet flowers; even with headlights on, the road was barely visible. Then down the other side, with the skies slowly clearing, the wet beads on every roadside leaf replaced first by red mud and then red dust until we came out at last into enormous fields of wheat and barley in which modern harvesting machinery was standing, into villages and the ubiquitous roadside traffic of pedestrians and bicyclists and groups of people waiting for buses. This land turning scrubby and ugly ended at the top of a pass from which there was a wide view of Lake Manyara, a shining shield below, then down a long zigzagging road and we were in the tropics, five thousand feet below the rim and three thousand lower than the floor of the crater, in ground-water forest, and banana plantations, intense sun, and hothouse air.

Surprising changes of scenery (like the sand dune before Olduvai, our first sight of cloud forest) had the same tonic effect on us that arrivals did; however tired of driving or surfeited with looking we might be, we became reanimated with a magic excitement. In the dappled roadside glade we picked for a luncheon spot, the air was sweet and warm and full of brook talk; long vines, thick as a wrist, hung sheer from the tops of trees and we each selected our own to swing from while over our heads Sykes monkeys swung by their feet and peered curiously down at us. Bob went off to the nearby village and came back with fat little bananas, two inches long and about as thick through, to add to our bread and cheese and beer; Margaret and I set out the picnic things and spread rumpled jackets to sit on as if we were getting ready for a dinner party.

We were still eating the bananas, their flesh very firm and slippery and fragrant, when a mysterious small music added itself to the sound of the brook. It was so much a part of the air that it was impossible at first to tell from where it came, till, growing a little in volume, it approached us through the trees from across the stream, and the intense sun-and-shadow materialized the figure of a young man. Darker than a Masai and wearing no beads, only a poor sort of tunic, he came steadily toward us, playing on a homemade two-stringed instrument with a tin can for a sounding board — a meandering little tune, plaintive and sweet, with a persistent, primitive rhythm. Neither friendly nor hostile, saying nothing in response to our greeting, he seemed to be playing only for himself. His face had that open yet remote look of the mute; the noon sun, straight overhead, gave his dusky dark skin the bloom of a moth's wing. Should we *give* him something? Near a village he could use money and hadn't we had music with our meal? He seemed neither to expect the coins nor to be particularly impressed by them and when we saw him again in the market place later, still sawing away, he remained as impersonal and mysterious as before.

Mto Wa Mbu is a very old village on the site of a caravan stop; we found it a bewildering bustle after the cratered emptiness of Ngorongoro. There was a dilapidated post office, a modern dispensary and school, a bar and entertainment emporium, a bulging store with a bulging Indian storekeeper and a tailor, sitting at his sewing machine on the

porch, making and patching clothes for his waiting cus-
tomers. Out in the pitted and dusty oven of the street we
saw many types — Masai and Mbulu, the local tribe, some
East Indians and some people who wore rings in their noses.
Margaret and I were fascinated by the printed cottons in
the open-air market, displayed on a counter beside piles of

folded cloths, baskets and knives, flashlights and wire strainers. Elsewhere, beautiful tomatoes and papaws and huge hands of the little chubby bananas were spread out next to a table covered with smoked catfish; and there were two appalling butcher stalls hung with odds and ends: curtains of stringy fat, tongues, a few nearly stripped ribs — all swarming with flies. Wherever we went the same tall and outrageously handsome Masai, red hair rigidly curled as a statue's, beads around his upper arms and swinging from his ears, was there too — following us silently or else standing on one foot against a wall, ostentatiously waiting for us. Vain as a peacock, he turned down an offer of two shillings for his photograph and was not at all like our Masai friends of the crater, the Mara and Talek.

I began to feel dazed and giddy. At two in the afternoon we had already been in three landscapes as different as separate countries and in three distinct climates and we still had a fourth ahead of us: the dry desert scrub on the far shore of Lake Manyara where we were going to camp. "You won't like it much — at first," said Bob, who always understated, so of course we were quite ready to defend the location — a little back from the bare soda flats of the lake shore, dead-looking acacias and thorn trees standing about, saving their moisture by not putting out a leaf or a flower. Underfoot it was rockier than the poorest New England field, the rocks extremely curious: full of nodules and fossil-like lines, so that crossing them felt like walking across gigantic gray barnacles. The campsite tilted toward the lake; beyond that flat, shining sheet rose the thousand-foot escarpment of the Great Rift Valley and the Ngorongoro highlands from which we had come — one faint blue plane behind another, insubstantial as air in the afternoon dazzle. In the foreground stretched a pink reef of flamingos.

While tents were being put up we walked out into the gray rock wilderness, straight into a group of giraffes and a serval cat, like a small leopard, who started up from very near, his coat deep gold against the gray dust he kicked up running away. But the real marvel of that countryside is the baobab tree, a phenomenon of the vegetable world that seems part mineral and animal as well. From a distance it is a child's inept drawing of a tree — all huge, fat trunk with a few squiggles of bare branches coming out at the top; nearer, it takes on warm pink tones and a smooth bark which looks as if it were melting down the sides of the tree like wax down a bottle. One trunk we measured was sixty feet around; the surfaces, particularly where the branches sprout out, are so big they are more like cliffs and ledges and tops of boulders than anything growing. Stick a knife into the bark, it sinks in as if into the flesh of a melon and the seeds of the squash-shaped pod are moist and citrus-tasting and refreshing.

Between the solitary pylons of these great presences, most curious termite mounds stick up here and there out of the gray rocks. They are hard as rock themselves, high or higher than a man and sculptured into fantastic castle shapes; study one carefully and the eye loses all sense of dimension: you might be gazing at a whole Mont-Saint-Michel. One we stopped to examine was inhabited by a family of dwarf mongooses who poked their heads out of holes to look at us, dashed around, popping up from, down into, and all around the mound — fast as quicksilver, bright-eyed and inquisitive.

It was a terrible, forbidding land; the sun burned down,

wind whirled the dust and whenever the wind died the flies
came to life. Swathed in scarves, and walking with head
bent in order not to turn ankles on the awful rocks, plucked
at by two-inch thorns sticking out of every bush and tree, I
thought of the final lines of that poem "Wilderness":

> The rock says "Endure."
> The wind says "Pursue."
> The sun says "I will suck your bones
> And afterwards bury you."

Bury *me*, yes — but everything around me — animal and
plant, insect and bird, found its own niche and food and
lived its span. The baobab chose this barren soil ahead of
all others, and thorn trees locked their sap away until called
by rain; termites flourished and so mongooses had villages
just right for their uses to move into; lions — as we were
to see next day across the lake in the park — found the flies
as annoying as we did but learned to climb trees, and, having
fed on a kill, sprawled on branches twenty feet above the
ground where the flies were less fierce. The lake, too shallow
and soda-saturated for large fish, is just right for flamingo
and pelicans . . . the list is endless, just as The Great Imagination is never stopped: like the ocean coming in on shore,
it pours into every hole and cranny, fills every shape; the
only thing it abhors — a vacuum.

Sometimes looking down from the air I have had a sudden uncanny sense of how anatomic the earth's surface is
with its arteries and veins of streams, the breast and buttock
hills, the public hair of wooded mounds; all turf and grass
and growth is its skin; air and moisture keep it alive as they
do me. This corner of the earth around Lake Manyara has

too great extremes, is too violent to be compared to a body — or even, to our limited senses, to feel alive at all; it gives one instead a glimpse into its geological nature and the enormous changes, pressures and upheavals it has undergone. Those mountain ranges behind one another and no more solid-looking than sky are the volcanic Ngorongoro highlands; the long straight wall along the lake shore (with a hotel on top) which stretches away in both directions as far as the eye can see, is a scarp of the Great Rift Valley where the crust of the earth slipped a thousand feet down for the length of a continent. Here — on our side of the lake — is desert, but across from us and only three or four miles for a flamingo, is a ground-water forest of unimaginable luxuriousness, fed by streams which come underground all the way from the crater to gush out, dark and clear and cold, from the sides and bottom of the Rift wall. Groves of orchid-decorated trees, huge rhododendron and ferns, make a fresh, moist shade; in the open there are green feathery masses of papyrus and palm.

Into this land the Masai and their herds have fitted themselves too, even though they have to bring their cattle as far as ten miles a day for water. As we returned from the forest to our camp over the wide soda flats, a herd of five or six hundred were being driven along beside us — the animals close together in a narrow, orderly line, an impressive white bull, wearing a big bell around his neck, in the lead. Two herdsmen with dogs were at the head of the herd, two in the rear — long earth-colored capes flapping, spears held high, and as we passed they held up their free hands in a warm gay greeting. But that dust floating over them — shot through with smoky light, soft as a chiffon veil — was a sign of the menace hanging over all these lands where the pasturage is poor and thousands of hooves harrow the earth to dust. How sad! How ironic! That people who kill only marauding predators, but whose entire economy and wealth is their cattle, should be a threat to the food of antelopes and gazelle and so to the whole delicate and perfect balance!

We were sitting having tea when the herd came alongside camp and two of the herdsmen — boys in their teens — came striding across the flats to call. Their dog bounded along with them but they ordered him to stay behind which he did, sitting quiet and attentive throughout their visit, occasionally and as discreetly as possible closing the gap. The boys had great charm. We gave them candies, whose cellophane and foil wrappers entertained them; they pointed to Margaret's and my freshly made-up lips with good-natured amusement; they went into ecstasies of mirth when Bob showed them their faces in the car mirror — peered into and poked it, turned their heads this way and that. The magnifying side of a shaving mirror was the culminating excitement — that and the bottle of soda pop we gave them.

Finally, with great flair and style they said goodbye and walked away over the brutal rocks, vitality and springiness in every step, the dog — panting and wagging — picking his own way behind them. A rise of ground silhouetted them briefly against the blazing sky before they went from view and for those few moments the pride and dignity of their figures was an overwhelming sight. We do not see each other like that often. In the streets of our cities, among the human honeycombs of high-rise buildings and in all that noise, the most distinguished people, the dearest friends, shrink to almost nothing as they climb into a car or hurry to catch the light. This vast, unforgiving land — indifferent to man in such another way — and the great sky overhead, illuminate all his heroism and folly, smallness and grandeur.

Perhaps the very harshness of that gray rock wilderness was what taught us at last to move really quietly, to keep utterly still, and so to find one of the shyest and rarest antelopes. Once adjusted to noise-ridden, haste-imposing civilization, it takes time to unlearn these habits which must be cultivated in order to live in it efficiently and survive. In cities one has to press through distractions with a certain desensitized inattention, impervious yet focused as a torpedo on course, while in all that noise only a shout is heard, only the sensational attracts. Here, if you put a foot wrong on teetering stones or tindery twigs, if you formed words — even in a whisper — the small birds flew and your presence was announced for hundreds of yards around. It was like playing at Indians to stalk the animals; not uttering a word made one breathe more quietly and as little as possible. You became acutely aware of the phenomenon of breathing — even more, of being *breathed*. It is an awareness which takes away a lot of ego: suddenly you feel how joined to all creatures you are — as dependent as they on air and light and food; created, and preserved, by the same pervading energy. Deep inside "where the meanings are," you let go: discovering you are neither as much in charge as you thought, nor as separate, but just your own manifestation of creation as they are theirs.

The purple grenadier — a vivid, skittery little bird — let us come quite near; a "white-eye," his eye a black bead at the center of a big white sequin fastened onto the side of his head, sat on a twig and dipped and looked and stared; a robin chat sang. Then, directly in front of us — and how did it get there, when we didn't see it appear? — stood a magnificent antelope with great twisting horns, white stripes penciled down its sides. There is a lovely elegance and dignity in all gazelles and antelopes but this — the male lesser kudu — had a particularly aloof and aristocratic look. He stayed, a statue of attention, until a rash whisper or too-quick movement sent him rattling away across the stones. But a few minutes later and fifty yards farther, the female kudu stared at us through a break in the gray screen of brush — a mysterious face at a window.

The sky over the Rift wall was almost drained of light when we came out into the open again. Down by our tents the warm bright eye of our fire winked and sparkled; the boys were talking in low brook-voices. A strange noise from the lake turned our heads just as the whole reef of flamingos lifted like a sunset cloud off the reflected sky, climbed and wheeled with a sound of airplanes far off, rose higher and higher. We watched, unmoving, as they melted out of sight on half their circle and returned, flickering and pink, on the other. And then they were gone, wound away for good; where they had been the first star was lit and in the tree beside us a bat with great yellow wings unfastened himself from a branch.

IX

I HAD FORGOTTEN how, somewhere three quarters of the way through vacations, trips, holidays, one comes to a kind of nadir. The first delight, the early raptures of discovery have worn off; it is not yet near enough the end for the vivid and poignant impressions before taking leave. Almost any given space of time — even a single day — has this valley into which, it seems, one has to go down; we are then at our most vulnerable, at the same time that the atmosphere becomes heavily charged with forces which can't be identified or named — devils are loose. On summer afternoons it is the hour of thunderstorms; on family vacations it is when children are most intractable, parents at their wits' ends, marriages rock in the waves. Six o'clock in the evening is suicide hour.

All of us were too occupied with the moment, too entranced, to suspect any such valley existed here, so that of course we went all the deeper into it. Also, the day before and right at its edge, we danced on the peaks. I have mentioned our exhilaration on coming to new landscapes, and the peak of Ngurdoto was so unlike anything else we had seen that it stood by itself in our experience as it does in fact. Even now, remembering, I find it hard to believe that any such mountain exists — rising off the plain so steep yet delicate, its entire surface covered with trees and flowers, the forest opening at intervals on glimpses of near and far, on the fifteen-thousand-foot heights of Mount Meru across the depths of a calm pastoral valley.

We had driven off in our cloud of dust from the dry plain and the baobab trees till outside Arusha a new kind of Masai village replaced the low dung huts in their wreath of thorn bush — these had high green hedges and circular thatch-roofed huts; their owners were out cultivating fields. Having passed down avenues of flame trees, between coffee and banana plantations and beautifully parked roadsides bordered with luxuriant canna, we were abruptly in the African part of town with its festival of color — a woman walking along wearing orange and purple, another in mustard and peacock blue, one in fuchsia and lime — all carrying large jars or petrol tins on their heads and babies in slings on their backs, holding themselves like caryatids. (What these women do with two lengths of cheap cotton cloth — one

worn as a skirt, the other as a shawl or hood — shows a
sense of style and color which shames most other women,
while in that sun the colors seem to glow with a light of
their own and washing and fading give them a rich matte
bloom.)

For a week Arusha had been a goal so that when we had
left the car in the western part of town near shops and
arcades, we rushed off to post office, camera and drug stores,
as flustered and excited as driven poultry. Lunch at the
new Arusha Hotel was very gay and the building endeared
itself to me with its plain, high-ceilinged rooms and jumble
of wicker furniture, its utter lack of pretense and modernity.
In a world where hotels are getting alike as airplanes or
automobiles and ostentatious as government buildings, this
looked and felt like the small European hotels of the early
part of the century. In the airy white dining room — windows open on a garden — we picked out our own dishes
from a long cold buffet, laughingly rubbed napkins and
tablecloth between our fingers, had half-bottles of a delicate
French wine.

All afternoon we moved through a steady crescendo of
discoveries, surprises, delight. Our campsite, a few miles
out of town on the curve of a rushing stream, was fresh and
green and more intimate than any other had been, partly
walled in by an overhanging cliff all green and quivering
with maidenhair fern. The water was peaty brown yet clear;
it talked in a wide range of voices and was like a trout stream
in a northern forest. In a fast-running part of it where reflected sunlight flickered up on the ferny wall, we bathed
away the dust and the desert, the closed-in feeling of having
worn all those clothes against the crater's cold; not since

Sand River had we had this luxury. After tea, we drove up
to the Ngurdoto crater.

Though I have never been to the South Seas, pictures of
those islands with their steep verdant peaks resemble what
we now climbed. Here was an altogether new aspect of
Africa — magnificent forests of giant podocarpus and trees
as large as our smaller redwood, the slopes under them
closely carpeted with a glossy ground-cover bearing mauve-
pink flowers like small orchids, their petals creamy thick as
a gardenia's. A single track of moist red earth printed into
this carpet winds up the western slope of the mountain to
its peak. Along here, the crater rim is some fifteen hundred
feet above its floor; on the farther side it has collapsed into
low hills. Once we had entered the gate — for this had
recently been opened as a park — we didn't see another soul
all afternoon; we might have been alone in Eden. Among
the big trees it was cool and fresh as dawn, the sound of our
engine almost completely muffled by the soft thick vegetation, the quiet jeweled with bird voices.

A little way into the forest we met a troop of colobus
monkeys, the shyest and most acrobatic of the tree people.
Moving with great rapidity and skill they travel through the
forest, going out to the very ends of branches and hurling
themselves into the air, to land with a great curtsying and
swishing of boughs on a tree twenty or thirty feet away. All
their lives they seldom go near the ground. They are stun-
ning to look at: black with a white fringe draped low across
the back, like an academic hood, tails a long bush of pure
white, thicker than a fox's brush, and black faces severely
framed in white, as though they wore the closest-fitting of
nun's coifs. The whole effect is so striking that you will find

more and more of them in specialty shops — made into pillow covers and fancy little rugs.

The family we found looked like so many fruit on the huge tree from which, one after another, they launched themselves to a smaller, lower tree and then on into the forest. A mother with a small baby came last. She took the same route up to a point where she stopped to consider the situation, giving quick anxious glances at the infant behind her, then she climbed up to a crotch and waited. He didn't join her. We had almost forgotten him when he suddenly made up his mind and without any hesitation followed where the rest of the tribe had gone — his tiny figure sailing out across the same abyss, his mother now behind him. Mythlike creatures they seemed; exotic as birds of paradise and a little catlike; at the furthest remove from apes and baboons, living like that in the air and the beautiful high trees. When their last rustling had died away, the forest was very silent, very full of their absence.

At a dip in the ridge we left the car and climbed up the steep green tunnel of a path to a little open peak. Far below, the crater floor lay like a golf green, dotted with trees and crossed by braiding and interweaving animal paths. Down there where no person is allowed to go, hundreds of buffalo laid their shadows along the turf and feeding giraffes stood wreathed in foliage; we could even make out dots of baboons and little running blobs which were wart hogs and a couple of rhino — pale gray rocks moving slowly about. All this we saw from an emerald pinnacle just big enough at the top to hold the five of us sitting on it in a thick carpet of leaves, a magical cone where one looked out in one direction at Mount Meru and in the opposite direction, suspended like a wisp of cloud in mid-sky and pale as the moon by day, at the very top of Mount Kilimanjaro.

The higher we drove along the track, the greater grew the trees, soaring at last so far up that looking into their crowns hurt one's neck; their trunks — of the same reddish tinge as the earth — were as big around as the most massive cathedral pillars. The sun, getting low now, cast barely slanted beams between them, turning everything in their path honey-gold. Just below the summit we stepped out onto a soft springy floor pooled with water from showers and climbed another green tunnel. Coming out onto that topmost pinnacle which was green and flowery as the other, it was as cold and blazing clear as if we were invading the sky. The only sound up there was a bee. Deep in the blue silence over our heads a strange scene was taking place between two birds, a peregrine falcon and a smaller hawk. It looked like an aerial battle. Over and over the small bird dove at the peregrine who then rolled neatly and swiftly onto its back, apparently to defend itself by thrusting back with its claws. Or so we thought, watching; not until we were in Nairobi again and on our way back to the world did we find out that what we had seen was the mating flight of the peregrine falcon who turns on her back to meet her mate face to face.

In that aerial setting, beneath that drama, we were all extraordinarily happy — bathed in a clarity of spirit as well as light. The steep little pinnacle which was our only foothold on earth was a point of balance between the near leaf and the far mountains, each equally clear and full of meaning — like the limpid little scenes beyond the shoulder of a Florentine madonna. Glancing at the others, I saw on their faces an expression of the most subtle joy — very alive and at the same time peaceful. It made me think of the look on the finest representations of Buddha who, at the heart of serenity, is totally alert and at one with the secret energy of earth and life.

Often, since then, I have thought about the almost sublime quality of that place and afternoon — a heightened version of so many we were experiencing — and how deeply they differed from other exhilarating hours in natural settings. Here, every landscape, every hour of the day was life-enhanced; elsewhere no matter how wild and lovely the place — if it lacked animals and birds one entire dimension was missing: it was dead. Ngurdoto was not only richly inhabited, it was beautiful as well. And we saw it better for being more attuned — more practiced by now in the way we were living. That constant openness to change and unknowns, the freedom from any role or image of ourselves and each other, was giving us an awareness, a spontaneity, which civilized life seems to suffocate. It came close to that state of "choiceless awareness" of which mystics speak; contemplating a pride of lions or a troop of monkeys was a kind of religious meditation: creation contemplating itself. Yet how much of my life — as those of others like me — is spent in surroundings and circumstances I must virtually shut out in order to survive! Sometimes it seems I am most rewarded for functioning like an efficient machine, snubbing the feeling-edge of consciousness, suppressing the delicate antennae of imagination and intuition. How else can I hold a car to a certain speed in a certain lane, move about in the concrete ant-palace of New York, do business on the telephone, by the clock? Never quite totally engaged in activities which demand so little of what makes me different from machines and computers, I find my aim becomes one of getting through with the task at hand and onto something else — not necessarily more interesting, but more related to what I am — in which as a human in a body, I can feel more at home.

Here we *were* at home, returned to the unity of creation from which we have been torn and so made whole again ourselves. Everything around us had evolved in its own uniqueness to its particular stage of life and consciousness — pink flowers at our feet and hundred-foot trees, the birds in their urgent ballet, those mysterious monkeys in their green aerial world. Even the shapes of the crater and its pinnacles were one stage in an infinitely longer-drawn-out process — if not "alive" at least having undergone tremendous changes and destined to continue doing so; nothing at all stood still, or apart; everything was part of the same dance. What we were experiencing was our part in the dance, in the balance of nature, discovering that if we stand outside it, it is we who are out of balance.

Yet there was something further about this one peak, this very place, which lifted the heart and tugged at the mind to understand: however mysterious this may sound, I have to say that it seemed to correspond, and in the most vivid manner, to a reality beyond itself and of a different order. This foothold on the earth and in the sky was a sign, asking to be known, and which only months later began to disclose something of its nature.

It grew suddenly colder. We drove down through the forest in the evening light, while across a valley the sun sank behind Mount Meru in a cold blaze of silver-lined cloud. Passing through layers of warm and cold air, as if through water, and standing in the open hatch, we had all the smells of the forest wafted to us — pungent, dank, aromatic, jasmine-sweet. Approaching a low-hanging branch or a leafy spray, we bent our knees and ducked; going around curves held more firmly to the car's frame; the engine, cool, not laboring, was barely audible from above. We passed another troop of colobus monkeys — these at their evening meal, daintily plucking and eating leaves, then swinging away into a neighboring tree to sample another foliage; at a turn in the road surprised, very close to, a little bushbuck who for a long time stood and stared at us, then glanced uncertainly down the steep slope which formed his escape, trying to decide between evils, not moving anything but his beautiful alert head. Finally he ducked down into the tunnel of green and we moved on down our own larger tunnel and out the park entrance where in the deepening dusk a dark figure stepped forward, saluting us, and the gate swung shut behind. The gate of Eden it felt like — with all that diversity and wholeness and harmony shut away now behind us in the night, the dance of eating and being eaten, creating and dying continuing undisturbed, as it has been since the beginning, was now but might not be forever. And we, with our knowledge and our divided minds, and our freedom — banished, hearing not the voice of Jehovah as he walked in the cool of the evening but — far more awfully — ourselves, asking the same towering question: Adam, where art thou?

That evening there was a certain irritability among us; something felt wrong. For the first time on the safari I dreaded the next day. Was it a reaction to the summit? Had that vision disillusioned us with our same old selves and so with one another?

A small group of people alone together and away from everything they are used to, is a highly delicate, organic structure — constantly changing in configuration, density, texture. If some outside force puts pressure on it somewhere, the whole shape alters; if one support is withdrawn, the fabric sustained by the others is strained at some points, at others collapses: it is like holding on to an edge of the most fluid blowy silk.

At one time or another each of us had let go of that fabric under the pressure of some unimportant but definite affliction, only Nat seeming tireless and irrepressible so that when, the morning after the peak, his turn came to feel badly it was like waking up to find a valley where a mountain had been. The drive that day was very hard — made more so by our concern for him and by his quietness. Dear Nat, usually the most voluble of the group: how we missed his cheerful, beaming ebullience and running commentary — those little sounds of "Aw — aw" he made at seeing Tommies — so caressing with their gentle downward inflection. He was not with us. He was somewhere very far away — and all of us were at that inexplicable nadir I have mentioned, hearts which had been lifted to such heights now low and uneasy.

The first hour, in poor farming country, was brightened by the beautiful sight of a group of women collecting soda from the shores of a soda lake, the brilliant colors of their clothing reflected in the water below the white line of soda, like vivid skaters on a winter pond; and the next, along the slopes of

Kilimanjaro, we drove through the richest grain country: past great stretches of gold wheat striped red-brown with new plowing; past long avenues of trees leading to big houses; private airstrips. Perhaps, after all, the day would be all right. Then we saw on the map that the thin line of a track diverged from the road we were on and would make a considerable short-cut to Amboseli. This being no day for a long drive, we decided to take it.

When things are going wrong, or relationships strained, it is easy to become superstitious and to read omens into all sorts of trifles. Appearances change their nature — as if the surface of life shivered and cracked open; weathers and places and even the light over them are strangely in accord with the inner situation. So the odd little settlement near the turnoff where we stopped for petrol was one of those places in a tale where mysterious instructions are given and not understood. Several buildings, messy as poor-white shacks in our own South, surrounded a dusty courtyard; dry, moribund coffee bushes struggled out of the red dust beyond and geese hissed and threatened next to a drunkenly leaning ark of a telephone booth. The place seemed to be run by a morose slatternly woman in her sixties who shuffled around in moccasins, looking pregnant and continually reproving an eager and abject husband. But beyond the house and its porch — where a jackal-like dog lay asleep on a broken-down sofa — a rose garden flowered in unbelievable abundance. Each plant grew out of a mound which held water in it as though it were a jar and the bare red earth between the mounds and between garden and house was being carefully swept by a boy with a brush broom: not a dead leaf or fallen petal or bit of debris was allowed to remain. The flowers had a prodigal, unearthly beauty as if the woman grafted all the care which might have gone to her person, family, house, onto these gigantic blooms, yet there was something faintly evil about them — they were *fleurs du mal.* I stared and stared at them as if they were messages to be decoded.

The track, when we found it, was scarcely even that. Near the main road it was dented with many human footprints and vaguely rutted but these became scarcer, dimmer until eventually it was a matter of getting down in any way we could off the slopes of the mountain, through rocks and scrub and dust to the plain below. Going, at most, five miles an hour we swayed and wallowed and plunged in a sea of desert vegetation, bracing ourselves as you do on a horse going down a steep slope, the heat growing constantly more intense. It didn't help to know that Bob had never come this way.

At the bottom of the slope lies the former lake bottom of Lake Amboseli — a totally flat floor of whitish clay, cracked with heat, bleached as bone. It is where meerschaum comes from; from a distance we saw the stuff heaped up around the mines. Getting down to the flat made us feel that now surely we must be near our destination but we still had miles to go across this curious desert, white dust pouring over us in thick clouds. There were trees of a sort — leafless or else shattered and broken by elephants, like trees blasted by heavy artillery fire. Zebras clattered about; Tommies stood in the stripe of shade made by a tree trunk. Mirages began to appear: shining lakes, always ahead, leading us on until, almost at the water's edge, the light sucked them away and there was nothing but more dry white clay and a farther shimmering illusion. Every line of trees or hint of green promised an oasis that wasn't there; Bob's mouth set in a tighter, thinner line until he finally found a little grass in a patch of shade and firmly said that this was where we were going to stop.

Maybe the beer was only cooler than that bone-white land but it still *seemed* touched with Ngurdoto's cold, its dry bitterness the only possible taste for that day. None of us ate much. In front of us, in the first hollow of land we'd seen in hours, the invisible swamp which sustained the grass we were sitting in, grew beds of papyrus — tall soft explosions of green in which an elephant stood up to its neck, delicately browsing. We were too tired, too concerned with the unfamiliar presence of Nat's silence in our midst to give it more than a glance. A sad new tenderness existed between us, as if we had all been shipwrecked and were protecting an injured, sleeping companion.

Our camp, when at last we reached it, was at the edge of an acacia grove, grown waist-high under the trees with Sodom apples — a weed now bearing its poisonous orange fruit the size of crab apples. It was one of the few groves for miles around. There were thin lines of trees — dongas — but between them there wasn't even the burnt grass of the Serengeti — there was nothing at all: what brings game to Amboseli is its occasional swamps, their water come all the way down from the snows of Kilimanjaro twenty miles away. Here elephants drink and bathe, waterbirds congregate and in the deeper pools hippo lie submerged to their eyes. Plains animals come from miles off for water — and so do the Masai, driving their herds.

When we went out later, looking for game, Nat stayed behind in camp, the only time of the whole trip he was to do so. It was just as well, for had he been with us he would have felt worse still. We had hardly left camp when we came to the first herd of cattle in the road ahead — the herdsmen sending them to both sides to let us through, the hundreds of animals all but swallowed from sight in the dust they raised. When we came to a second and third herd, Bob turned off on another road but they were all the same: for the next three quarters of an hour we drove through and past herds of cattle — each one in a blizzard of dust, the herdsmen standing or walking as if in a great storm and the ground so printed and plowed by hooves it no longer seemed like ground at all but a moving, swirling cloud. Even inside the Land Rover with the windows screwed up we choked on it, it swirled through the car's interior, got into eyes, ears, nose. I began to cough, my chest heavy as if with bronchitis. How did they stand it out there, those Masai? Sometimes one held his cape across his face but mostly they were busy driving the cattle, waving sticks or spears, running after a maverick. A very few waved but mostly the men looked driven, too, and why not? On every road, dust plumes spiraled upward, each one from a tourist car out like ourselves scattering herds and boiling up still more of those deadly white clouds. And the game? There was scarcely a grass-blade to eat: if any struggled up through those lifeless drifts it would be pulverized by hooves; the fine network of roots just under the surface which even in the driest season holds life safe from the sun, was being chopped to shreds. That network supports all the wild herds: their grazing teeth cultivate its tops; because of predators it is never overgrazed. What everywhere else combined into a dance of life was — here — a *Totentanz* of wild game, Masai, tourists — the outsiders come to see the animals; animals come for water; herds, also after water, trampling the animals' food to death.

After the morning's hard drive and missing Nat, it became almost too much to be borne, until right in the middle of the drought, the desert, the despair, appeared a limpid blue pool fringed with reeds, alive with birds. Out in the middle of it, four hippos were playing like porpoises — wet and slippery and wiggling water out of their silly ears, diving and sliding in and out of the ripples. Two surfaced at once, facing one another, and kissed — a great, affectionate, toothy kiss. So often things seemed to turn out this way: just when everything most dreadful about this continent had nearly obliterated the rest, a pool of purest delight offered its refreshment.

And then came the mountain. All day while we crept around its base it had remained in the clouds; now it slowly emerged — the white ice-cliffs at the summit first — a stationary cloud-platform floating an impossible sixteen thousand feet in the air above where we stood. It hung there unreal and detached, separated from its own base by a cloud mass as blue and hazy as the sky. With great majesty the upper slopes then slowly freed themselves, their outlines came clear. The sun, setting, ignited the clouds, separated them, one from another, turned them into rosy and fiery, swirling and plumed presences — an apocalyptic vision, a soundless symphony. When the sun had gone farther down, the presences turned back into a gray wall, the ice cliffs hung a few minutes longer like a suspended crown, then they dissolved, utterly, into space.

We turned away and drove back in the dusk, not saying

much, and ate our dinner under the stars. There were more stars than I have ever seen anywhere — and Venus setting, pink as a wild rose, right down at the end of the road.

Next morning the mountain was again invisible but it is a peak you are very much aware of whether you see it or not. I have never known a presence like it. Most mountains are part of a range; Fuji's ascent from its surrounding is so uniform and gentle it still belongs to the land from which it rises. Kilimanjaro, more than a third again as high, feels like a sky rather than an earth phenomenon; you feel yourself paying it the repeated homage of looking to see whether it is there, or how much of it, or what its appearance is in some particular light. Perhaps if you lived a long time at its feet you would lose some of this awareness, though I doubt it.

The other great thing at Amboseli is the light. There is something in the air, as at Delos, a quality of reflection off the white earth, and the uninterrupted levelness of land which makes every animal and bird stand out in a glory of detail. Each encounter, even with zebra and gazelles, showed us the animals more clearly than we had yet seen them: the delicate demarcations of beige on the sides of Grant's gazelle revealed their subtlest differences, one saw the black line up through the eye which gives them their slightly wistful, melancholy expression; and a large herd of elephants we found near camp and moving our way were sculptured in such clean lines that ears lay over sides and animals were seen against one another like some sharp abstract of overlapping gray panels.

Yet that light was overwhelming, too; we felt so overpowered that even with a spectacular campsite and Nat beginning to get better we longed to get away and decided to leave early. There was violence in the air.

The last night was ridden with demons. The great tide of elephants which, unless it changed direction would come right by us, was moving steadily our way when the sun went down and it grew too dark to distinguish their shapes. As we got ready for the night and for a predawn departure, we kept stepping out of our tents, trying to make out just where they were. All evening the wind rose; our campfire blew to a hot white, streamed sparks like a Fourth of July fireworks display and through the rising noise one heard the elephants trumpeting — that terrifying roar split into a scream which is as elemental as if the ground were breaking open and giving birth. Just at nightfall a whole herd of frightened impala streamed by within a few feet of us, almost knocking over tables and chairs in their flight.

By the time we went to bed the wind was howling and had built up to a near gale; Bob went about securing tent pegs; we all made things fast as if for a night at sea. Still it increased, roaring in the trees over our heads, sighing through mosquito netting, flapping and thundering canvas. Unable to sleep I got up and checked fastenings in the outer part of the tent and Bob, seeing my light, came over to see if everything was all right; though his tent was lit up as usual and shone like a glowworm, he was moving all around camp, checking and putting things away. I stayed at our small window, looking out; the stars were burning with furious brilliance, appearing and disappearing behind rock-ing branches; then headlights swung over and down the trunks of trees and a car drove into camp: it was a man by himself, lost, asking the way to the lodge. Bob gave him

directions but urged him to turn back and take the longer way around: the elephants were still there, very close, screaming from time to time into the wind.

Unbearably restless and excited I went out into the gale, clothes plastered against or whipping my skin. In place of the enormous silence of most nights there was this other immensity in which everything, including elephants, was torn loose, pulled, forced and driven. I have been out in gales, even hurricanes, before but never felt more powerfully the assault of elemental violence, not just on the senses but on my whole being: there was an urgency upon me like physical passion: I was blown to a white intensity like the fire, earlier, which had now been quenched. I walked out from under the trees to look for Kilimanjaro but though the sky was so violently clear, no mountain at all was to be seen: where it seemed to me it should have been, there were only those other worlds — pronged with spears of light.

By morning everything was serene, still, swept utterly clean. When dawn came, the mountain soared up in all its regal dignity — every fold of its slopes visible; the ice cliffs at the summit — like sugared frosting dripping down the sides — turned pink in the sunrise, but by that time we were well on our way, crossing the lake bottom, fleeing from whatever evil it was that had assailed us.

X

On large-scale maps of East Africa, Kilimanjaro and Mount Kenya, Mount Meru and Ngurdoto show as dark circles of very high altitude rising out of a pale plain of nearly uniform level, like islands out of the sea. Ecologically they *are* islands, a fact of the greatest mystery to botanists and zoologists since how, then, did their species originate? The birds and animals which inhabit them and the plants growing out of them, though they may be identical at the same altitude on different mountains, cannot migrate from one to the other; they are cut off as if by thousands of miles of ocean since between "islands" there is nothing to sustain their particular lives. Death by starvation or drought or enemy surrounds each mountain world as completely as the ocean isolates the land and each mountain *is* a world, marvelously self-sustaining at every level and in harmony at all points. We had been in that world-inside-a-world of the Ngorongoro Crater; climbed the pinnacle of Ngurdoto; fled from the discord of Amboseli; now — in the Aberdares — we were to climb up through mountain forest and camp in the high moor country at ten thousand feet.

The Aberdares, and the whole north frontier country beyond, had a particular fascination for Bob so that long before we went there he had told us things about them. They were hard to put together — those giant groundsel and dwarf trees he described; miles of tussock grass and a black leopard running between them, and elephants — right up to twelve thousand feet. It seems that elephants with their extreme delicacy of movement are fine mountaineers who have an accurate sense of gradients; presumably Hannibal knew what he was doing.

Amboseli and the Aberdares were separated for us by an afternoon and night in Nairobi. They felt terribly unreal — the city which had seemed very small after Rome and New York was now huge and bewildering, and lunch at the Norfolk Hotel among all those well-dressed people a dizzying experience. There was so much sound everywhere after the deep quiet, and the gasoline fumes felt thick and poisonous to breathe; they were the first thing we noticed on nearing the city across the plains south of it, after factory chimneys,

railways and gasoline pumps — all the ugliness which surfaces in the wake of industry.

But in the afternoon we visited Isak Dinesen's, or Karen
Blixen's, house — we made a pilgrimage there. What had
been her enormous acreage of coffee plantation, native sham-
bas and forest was now much reduced in size and surrounded by country estates and suburban villas but the trees
and lawn, the view across to the Ngong Hills, were still
exactly as she describes them in *Out of Africa*. I knew from
the book where the rooms would be and the two millstones
out on that brick terrace where she used to sit and listen to
her people's troubles and examine their sick; but what I was
not prepared for was the very Danish appearance of the
house with its red tile roof and its windows low to the
ground and grouped together as they have been in Danish
farmhouses since the twelfth century. The house was being
used for a domestic science school and since there were no
students there at the moment, the directress — caught off
guard, perhaps, by my addressing her in her native Danish
— let us see the downstairs. Very few of the baroness' fur-
nishings remained but a great deal of her presence did —
or was that my imagination and the spell which even her
memory casts? You had only to see that gaunt and passion-
ate face — at once old as Egypt, beautiful and ageless —
and the burning eyes continued to look out at you from the
deep pool of all human experience, having seen and suffered
all, judging nothing. It was this huge impartiality of hers
which overpowered us. The young woman who flew over
the wilds in a small plane and hunted marauding lions in
the dark, who bandaged up a child screaming from fatal
gunshot wounds and fed sugar lumps to a pet bushbuck, had

come to terms with the goddess Kali, our universal mother-destroyer; Karen, too, showed you the sword in one hand, the flower in the other — to her they were equal marvels. *Life is both*, she said, somewhere between the words of her magical language and the sounds of her deep voice, and suddenly good and evil and all the opposites were reconciled; the self-imposed judgments and restrictions and terrors melted away in tears. She was the ageless, detached mother none of us have.

Now I sat at one of the two millstone tables and thought of her. A cypress which must have doubled its height since her time cast a deep sundial shadow along the rough stones which were as red as the African soil. Overhead moved the clouds she so loved — those clouds which never congregate into the great towering accumulations one sees over our Continental Divide, but drift in endless herds from over the edge of the world, emphasizing distances by their advancing or retreating planes, laying blue shadows on the tawny grass. In the middle of the millstones someone had planted clumps of white phlox; the little round towers of its bloom blew about in the afternoon wind. And across there on the Ngong hills, where the land juts out from the second peak in a sort of terrace, lay Denys Finch-Hatton and I thought of his grave and the lions coming there.

From "Karen" we went to have tea with a charming American couple who had moved from Boston to Kenya to see what could be done about saving the wildlife. Frank Minot had called on us when we first arrived in Nairobi and we had had an enlightening talk, sitting out on the balcony of our room which was filled with piles of clothing being sorted for departure. He had just returned from working with Joy

Adamson's husband at teaching two partially tame lion cubs
— the ones used in the film of *Born Free* — to hunt for themselves. "It's a serious business, making pets of lion cubs and
letting them go," he said, "because then you must make it
up to them and teach them how to get along in the wilds."
The cub they called "She" now weighed two hundred and
fifty pounds yet still delighted in throwing herself exuber-
antly at one or another of the two men, knocking them flat.
"I just can't take that sort of thing," Frank said, ruefully
rubbing a sore shoulder. "Well," (he went on) "we all get
a bit crazy out here in Africa — maybe it's the altitude or
something." But there was nothing crazy about the clear and
orderly account he gave us of the situation in conservation.
There was one area which he felt might make a very valu-
able park; while we were on safari he had promised to complete a report of it and it was this we were now going to see
him about.

The Minots' house, like Karen Blixen's, looked out over a
sloping lawn and a little valley to those four peaks which
arrange themselves into such a classic composition, leading
the eye there and giving it something to rest on. Near the
front door a garden full of tea roses was fenced in to keep the
bushbuck from trampling and eating them and to keep the
leopards from following the bushbuck. In a living room with
many touches of old Boston in it — whaling prints and maple
rockers and Paul Revere silver — the men sat and talked
while I chatted with our hostess — a calm, gentle young
woman brought up in Cambridge, Massachusetts, and on
Cape Cod. She knew and loved Martha's Vineyard where
we usually summered and asked me: didn't I miss being at
the island? A beautiful, tiny five-year-old daughter tripped

in and out of the room wearing her eighteen-year-old sister's heeled slippers; a cat, half tabby, half Siamese, jumped on and off chairs and whirled, tail high, through the room while the men talked and a grandfather clock in the corner slowly and heavily ticked away.

Setting out again from Nairobi next day was the beginning of another loop of a spiral: we had done all this before — very long ago it seemed — so that everything was the same yet entirely different. The same shoes and sweaters and bush jackets had become wrinkled as an old face. Nat's hat was like some exotic convoluted shell; we knew one another now, in health and sickness, fresh and tired, at dawn and dark. We knew what to expect, having learned that all ex-pectation was misleading since bird walks led to elephants and peaks to depression. Starting on our last week of safari, our last days together, we entered the void again with the enormous change that we now recognized it for what it was.

At Nyeri, a lovely resort town at the edge of the Aber-dares, the weather report for the mountains was not good. The road in was marked as being open but Mount Kenya, across the plains, was invisible and dark clouds completely obscured where we were going. Amyas found a half inch of blue on the horizon and pointed out that that was where the wind was from, at which the rest of us teased him for his in-curable optimism. "Well, let's try it," said Bob.

We were in the country of the Kikuyu — a farming tribe who cultivate every square foot of hill and valley with maize, coffee, bananas, vegetables. They pasture their cattle along the sides of the road so that these are close-cut brilliant green grass, all tracked through with paths — the road and its banks a vivid red. For miles both sides of the road were

populated with streams of pedestrians and cattle, with Kikuyu women carrying staggering bundles of wood by slings
around their foreheads, and old men, many with a goat or
lamb on a string, wearing British army surplus overcoats
hanging around their ankles. A far cry from the elegant
Masai, yet we saw extremely lovely faces on the women and
a great deal of warmth and charm.

Once into the forest, the landscape grew steadily grander,
the conditions rapidly worse. There were the same giant
trees, glades and flowery ground cover as at Ngurdoto with
views across steep valleys to other forested slopes, which
exhilarated us in the same way. At nine thousand feet the
bamboo forest began and we entered an eerie, churchlike
gloom of green and silvery gray — the verticals of trunks
thrusting out of shiny satin-lined sheaths and fountaining
forty, fifty feet overhead into Gothic arches, all making a
curious creaking sound in the wind. It began to rain; the
road grew muddy, then slick, until we were continually skid-
ding — falling off into the bank at our left, half turning
around, while off to the right we tried not to look down into
abysses veiled by cloud and, in front, the windshield wipers
ground steadily away on a world shrunk to a dimly lit fan.
Crawling more and more slowly, holding our breath as we
crossed unfenced bridges over foaming rivers, we finally
came to our campsite on the Gikiruru River. It was inside a
rain cloud; a hundred feet was as far as you could see in any
direction; the way in from the road was between five-foot
gnome trees bearded with moss, vistas of wet moss and
grassy rooms stretching away underneath. As we stood
among the piles of tents and duffels and the boys started
making camp, a little red duiker — no bigger than a grey-

hound — tiptoed into the sopping grass at the edge of our vision and started to eat, then lifted its head and held it our way, ears stiffly cupped, wondering and speculating — a delicate receiving-set on the finest spindles. A blow on a tent peg sent it flying back into cloud but in a few moments it came cautiously back and for the rest of the time we were there browsed in the patch of grass at the edge of camp.

With what little light there was beginning to go, Nat labored at finding and drying out wood for a fire, arranging it as if designing a whole building, nursing the faintest promise of a flame. And later, in our tent, inside the dripping canvas, we had steak with mashed potatoes and spinach and a bottle of red French wine. Miles overhead in the middle of the night, a jet bored its way toward its destination — probably the flight from Rome to Nairobi. It was the first time in nearly a month I had heard that sound.

Even before I opened my eyes next morning the lids felt warm and bright and the first thing I saw was the rich orange glow of sun through the canvas. Outside there was a blazing blue sky and the tent poles and grass in the tent's shadow were white and spiky with frost. A few miles from the Equator, we remembered, and in August, warming our hands around cups of steaming tea, coat collars turned up! On three sides of the high shelf on which we were camped, open moor stretched away for miles, broken only by patches of darker green heath, or rising here and there into bizarre peaks; on the fourth side were the dwarf woods, trunks black with moisture, sunlight now slanting into exquisitely landscaped gardens of diminutive flowers. In the brilliant silence, the waterfall a quarter of a mile downhill made a warm deep sound.

The moors were very strange with their enormous tussocks — great radiating spheres of grasses sparkling with flashing colored globes of water, the spheres so solid at the core that you had either to walk around them or take giant's steps up and over them. Bob looked at them unhappily. "Pity it's so wet," he said, "you've no idea how wonderful this grass is to lie in — each tussock is a couch you sink into." But to walk in it was terrible and we came back to breakfast after our early walk exhausted.

It was the last we were to see of the sun, for the day went from cloudy to foggy, rain, thunderstorms — clouds streaming from out of an apparently bottomless cauldron beyond the far ridge or blowing like smoke from a huge invisible fire somewhere down on the earth. Amyas went down to the river and caught two brown trout at the foot of the falls where celadon green moss hung from the trees and fog drifted over the stream. On the opposite bank giant groundsel rose fifteen feet in the air and red-hot poker flowers burned upward on their naked stalks. The river was wide and smooth at the falls, rolling in a glassy curve over an edge as straight and level as a stage. The front wall of this stage curved inward so that behind the curtain of falling water was a space several feet wide and a rocky shelf dripping with swaying ferns and moss. You could go in there, I thought, and keep dry and hidden, and I saw now how Laurens van der Post's grandmother was saved as an infant from the massacre which took her parents' lives when her nurse hid with her by day for a whole week in just such a place as this.

It was a strange day we spent in that country of heath and cloud — Bob unhappy that we weren't able to see his

beloved Aberdares and all of us anxious about getting out,
for how, after still more rain and no sun to dry out the earth,
were the Land Rovers going to move? In the afternoon Bob
and Amyas and I squelched and slithered up the road on
foot, meeting near the unfenced bridge a man walking with
an African servant who was holding a length of rope and a
shovel. I couldn't place his accent when he addressed us
but it sounded vaguely Italian. His build was solid and
stocky; he looked dazed with fatigue. He asked if we'd seen
a Land Rover and we said no, that we had two but that they
hadn't moved today.

"I've lost my friend," he explained. "We were to meet up
there" (he pointed south, toward the gate going out of the
park) "but when he didn't come last night, I got worried and
walked down after him — no use going in *my* Land Rover."

"Where's yours?"

He pointed in the other direction, along the road we'd
come in on. It was stuck, he explained.

"You walked, in that weather? In the dark?"

"Yes. Down to the Rohuruini Gate."

"But that's seven miles!"

"Yes. I think I walked about fifteen miles. When I
couldn't find him I decided I'd missed him and came back
up."

He smiled in a vague way and looked around, as if his
friend might be hiding, behind a tussock.

There was a low chattering sound and a Land Rover,
headed our way, crossed the bridge. We watched without a
word as it struggled up the hill on our side, skidded, vanished from view around a curve and reappeared; once it got
mired and two men got out and pushed it. When it finally

reached us, we saw the words "Diocese of Nyeri" painted on the side. Tired as they were the two friends embraced and broke into a stream of Italian of which it was possible to catch only a little. How they had missed one another was a mystery they couldn't bother to explain as they hurriedly said goodbye to us and drove off. We watched them — priests, we decided, on a visit to a mission — as they slithered and slid away across the moorland, getting stuck, getting out and pushing, finally going out of sight over the ridge.

We walked up to the ridge ourselves and then out into the moor where for half an hour or more we stood in the drifting fog, watching the beautiful changing light, the vanishing and reappearing distances and — in a saucer of a tarn below us — one lone little grebe swimming about in the watery clouds. Sometimes the gray scud going by overhead was darker, and appeared more solid, than the misty moor below so that all sense of orientation was gone and we might have been suspended upside down from clouds; at others, the gray canopy lifted and parted over openings of tenderest blue penetrated by a jagged tooth of rock. The mist was a soft brush on our cheeks; hair and eyelashes were festooned with beads.

Through his binoculars — for he never stopped looking for distant things — Bob discovered far off in the grass tussocks an emerald bog which we went to explore — an exquisite little world twenty feet long and half as wide which made a deep dimple in the ground and was entirely carpeted with a light moss thickly set with small flowers. One of these was very much like our arbutus and had a similar fragrance; another — no larger than the head of a pin — had the intense luminous blue of some tropical fish and there were little flat daisies, white and yellow, all of them tightly buttoned into the green stars of moss. What a place when the sun shone! What a royal bed! Getting down into it was like going into a *mille-fleurs* tapestry: there should have been a seated lady with a falcon on her wrist, a unicorn standing above her. Kneeling in my sodden and muddy clothes I felt elated, my heart full and round as that heart the lady of the tapestry holds out in her aristocratic fingers. Bob touched my shoulder and pointed: on a higher ridge, in sharp silhouette against a patch of blue, were the heads of two waterbuck, ears wide as open flowers, watching us with motionless attention.

The next morning, when it was once more clear and we decided after a few hours of sun to try and get off the mountain, I went out for a walk alone. On the way down to the waterfall through thick patches of impenetrable heath I was careful to sing out as Bob had taught us to do "to tell any buffalo who might be around" that I was there, but although fresh elephant tracks pitted the earth near the pool where Amyas had caught his trout, no animal stirred. In the clear, magnifying light, the scale of things was fascinating: I might have been a giant striding over the earth's streaked and cloud-shadowed surface or an insect in a grass patch, for how could sizes be judged where clumps of vegetation on the moor could as well have been tall forest as low bushes and whole minutely detailed landscapes were crossed at one step?

And what *shapes* there were! Stars and rosettes of thistle; fountains of fern; spires of blue-green ground cover; soft fireworks explosions of grass; green and yellow busbies.

Plants thrust, sprayed, spread, wove mats, hung in festoons, made soft carpets.

It was wonderful now to walk all soul alone. I had lost the last of my early fears and uneasiness and grown new awarenesses — as if out of my body and skin fine new senses extended like cilia. I saw and heard, felt and smelled with what I can only call a generalized acuteness and had, too, a new appreciation of the animals' dignity — their right to their country and how I was there as an outsider, a guest. I longed to see the black leopard Bob had encountered on his last trip here, or else come upon the strange sight of elephant — apparently on a Scottish grouse-moor — but the only creatures about were a few far-off waterbuck moving quietly among the tussocks. In the grass under the lichen-encrusted trees lay a little pile of guts — presumably from a small animal since there were no feathers about: whatever had killed there had removed them so neatly and expertly not a membrane was broken and their beautiful soft colors shone in the sun. But the only definite sign of the leopard was one of his turds being consumed by masses of glittering dung beetles; what they didn't need to nourish themselves they would use as a place in which to lay their eggs so that the larvae would be kept warm and hatch, later, into a food supply. What incredible cleanliness, economy, design! Everything constantly rotating: feeding and being fed on; consuming and eliminating! No wonder nature is undying — it feeds on itself.

Leaving, we walked the first mile; tried riding in the Land Rover but were promptly mired and so alternately walked and drove until we were out of the cloud world. Halfway down we passed the great salt lick to which the bongo,

largest of the antelopes, come at night; the bare, pock-
marked ground was carpeted with redheaded green parrots.
"Be very careful along here," Bob warned Amyas and me
as we walked on ahead. "Animals may come down the slope
and try to cross the road to get to the salt lick. Keep an eye
open." A few minutes later there was a cracking of branches,
a loud hollow bark and a bushbuck galloped out of cover
and in again; a chattering monkey darted out of his way.
And almost at the Rohuruini Gate a giant forest hog right
out of a medieval hunting scene trotted across the road in
front of us, so close the naked skin showed pink between
the bristles and we saw the way his tusks overlay his lip.
Another mile and we were back among Kikuyu farms and
villages, moving slowly along in the patient river of pedestrians and domestic animals; we were out of the Aberdares.

There were four days left — four days for that north country which brought a special tone to Bob's voice, a rapt look
to his eye. But it wasn't safe to camp there and there was
only one place where we were allowed to go — the Samburu
Game Reserve — for marauding bands of *shifta* — bandits
— were looting, terrorizing, and killing and, what was worse,
were moving about and turning up in unexpected places.
We would stay for the first and only time at a lodge. Very
sadly we said goodbye to Njorogi, Ngugi and to Kimani who,
to the end, accepted all compliments, all comments with his
smiling *Ndeos,* and watched them drive away in the Land
Rover; it was a helpless, abandoned feeling that flowed in
when the road was empty again behind them.

Driving by ourselves through the beautiful rich farmland
on the slopes of Mount Kenya, we tried to find out more

about the shifta. It seemed there had always been a certain amount of intertribal banditry in this country, some tribes coming from as far as southern Ethiopia on plundering raids. This was now aggravated by terrorism arising from political tensions with Somaliland: the Somalis, feeling that the northeastern corner of Kenya was by right theirs, were instigating and carrying out raids of their own: whole villages were wiped out. Near our destination there was a little settlement called Archer's Post which was now mostly peopled by the survivors of a particularly successful massacre.

We asked Bob about the intertribal looting. What did the shifta want?

"Testicles."

"*What?*"

"Yes. To hang around their necks, dried. Or from bracelets."

When there was livestock, he added, they took that.

We crossed the Equator, drove through the pretty little town of Nanyuki, went on. Nearing the north country was like approaching the sea: in some indefinable manner the wonderful sense of a different degree of space, the lower and more extended horizon ahead, announced itself long before the land came to an end. And there at the edge of a shelf it lay — all immense, level distance, several thousand feet lower than where we were, and mountains rising out of the plain in such curious shapes that they looked fabulously old and worn, deeply mysterious. Beyond the farthest mountains, you felt a wider ocean of land stretch away under a still fiercer sun.

At Isiolo we stopped to get permits to cross the frontier; a large bulletin board showed all the main roads — Isiolo to

Meru, to Marsabit and Maralal, to Mado Gashi and Wajir — CLOSED. Only one, the road to Samburu, had the word "OPEN" after it.

While Bob called on officials in a series of small, neat white buildings, Margaret and I wandered about in the little park outside. It was the noon hour and in spite of a breeze very hot. A hedged-in space was jammed with a babbling, chattering crowd of people unlike any either of us had ever seen; we peered over the hedge to get a closer look. Their skin was almost dead black — having neither the bronze patina nor the crow-feather blue of other dark skins. They were small of stature with hard wiry builds, the women wore nothing but necklaces and a kind of half skirt, the men a

G-string. When Bob returned, we learned from him that they were Turkanas, a fine people who were going through hard times, their land turning to desert, their stock being stolen till some were reduced to living on wild fruit and palm nuts. Strong and self-reliant, they had beautiful songs which could be appreciated by Europeans, yet they were living like Stone Age men. Margaret and I looked at them as unbelievingly as they did us. Bob thought they were probably waiting for a court case, and who knew what they might have suffered? Yet I felt oddly shaken in their presence. Their appearance, their faces, were so primitive, so close to our common ancestors — those shadowy beings who had huddled around fires at Olduvai — that my whole usual image of people was jarred loose.

Months later Amyas confessed to me that he had been highly uneasy those last days. Perhaps I should have been, though what did worry me were those faces, and the thirty- or forty-mile drive between Isiolo and the reserve, through flat, burnt desert without a single settlement and only occasionally a lone figure or two with a few goats or cattle — Samburu, now, and not Masai. Enemy or friend — how did one know? What passion for land or wealth or equality, what volcanic resentments lay hidden under the dusty cape of that man with the sardonic face — what would he and his companion do if we had a flat and were stopped beside the road?

But then, crossing the Ewaso Nyiro River — which rises in the Aberdares — we were in the Reserve. Along the river grew doum palms with their trunks dividing into graceful lyrate Y's, like the horns of impala, their fronds curved over on themselves like those pleated paper fans one had for party favors as children. Off to the right sauntered a herd of animals new to us: the immensely stylish oryx — dove-gray with a black face, black garters and three-foot straight horns that sweep back like steeply raked masts. We passed a reticulated giraffe — glossy and dark as a ripe chestnut and covered all over with a fine white net of markings; and a herd of Grevy's zebra — more like horses than those in the south — less hippy, with bigger ears and finest black stripes on white instead of white on a lot of black. And then, in his extraordinary way, Bob, driving along, saw out of the corner of his eye a fantastic flower which we all got out to look at. *Caralluma retrospiciens* is a globe the size of a tennis ball completely covered with small, totally black rosettes having very dark red centers — the whole giving off a lemony scent and the florets edged with cilia which appear to have a life of their own: these were moving about without a breath of wind.

Since Isiolo we had driven along in anxious, even fearful silence. Each day we passed through a whole spectrum of moods, our relationships varying and shifting, though always around the frameworks of individual personality; they were the constants in the equations, the rocks around which flowed a constantly changing stream. Silences were of many kinds: meditative and contented, puzzled or critical, the silence of complete communion. Most often they burst into talk, and delight, after food; at unexpected new scenery, at arriving somewhere and now — after new scenery, new animals and trees and flowers we turned in at the lodge — a charming cluster of thatch-roofed buildings of natural stone, overlooking the river and shaded by giant trees full of monkeys and birds. Right on the river bank, our three adjoining *bandas* each had an enormous airy room open to the high thatch and a porch facing the river, which at this point is wide and majestic-looking in spite of the many sandy or muddy flats between channels of deep water. The trees along both banks were old and impressive, with the tenderest green foliage; a few yards beyond them all was harsh gray desert. On the grass outside our bandas, there were stone tables and seats and pools for birds; at our front door the golden baskets of weaverbird nests swung from the branches like oversize Christmas tree decorations shining against an intense turquoise sky.

When I sat out there, later, the birds were darting in and out of the entrances into their nests, whistling and calling, and a young vervet monkey came and shared the terrace with me, sitting on a stone stool across from me, glancing this way and that like a self-conscious child, never quite returning my look. His little black hands with their shiny black nails hung relaxed and unmoving over his feet; when he shifted position, he showed his rosy penis and blue balls which were as gaudy as the sky. Eventually he lay down full length on his stool, one hand over the stone edge, head turned my way, and we studied one another — I, over the tops of my glasses, he with his flat, sad monkey eyes, which for a long time didn't move from my face. In a zoo he would have seemed a prisoner and my pity for him would have balanced my repulsion. At close range, free, he wasn't repulsive at all but struck me as being pitiable in a far more profound way. Strange little homunculus — caricature of my kind — he was a prisoner of evolution, spared my failures and despairs but fated for ever and ever to do no more than to play and sleep and copulate in the trees and stuff fruit and nuts into himself with those unsuccessful hands. While for my kind — what might *not* happen? By what extraordinary plan, or amazing accident, by what *extra* energy at the core, had mind deepened and widened until it curved back on itself in self-scrutiny, wrote a *Divine Comedy*, composed symphonies, designed itself wings?

Now something about my little vervet made my heart turn with fear — something about the look of the hands, the face: in his monkey way he shook me just as had the Turkanas, long ago this morning. Someone has written of being told by a very old Masai chieftain, "But we *must* wear our beads — how else could we be told apart from the animals?" To think there are people that near to Eden, living in the same historical time with us! Maybe my awe, then my dismay — thinking of the menace we become to ourselves, and so to each other, with every successive step away — maybe this went out mysteriously into the air outside me, for with no manifest reason the monkey jumped to his feet, laid his tail over his wrist like a lady carrying her train, and disappeared over the bank.

XI

THE IMMENSE JOURNEY was coming to an end, though in a deeper sense I am sure that as long as any of the five of us lives, it will continue its existence somewhere, separated from the present moment only by the mirage of time. And since the last days of an experience intensify it, toward the end we felt more than ever connected to life, nearer the heart of the mystery.

The land itself participated — inviting exploration, at the same time that it was rich with secrets. At this point it seems unlikely that I shall ever go farther into that north country of Kenya but I do not mind; besides, even if it were possible to see every land one wanted to, how terrible that would be! The magic of surmise, which is the parent of wonder, would be murdered. And we did see its promise.

Twice we got up at six and were out in time to watch the sunrise suffuse with color those curious mountains to the north. They are like no other mountains. The clarity of air, combined with the way they jut alternately and abruptly out of the surrounding country and are worn down to most strange elemental shapes, makes for a retreating perspective of distinct planes — like old-fashioned theater wings, like giant gates — while in the foreground, as clearly silhouetted against sky as our winter trees, the doum palms move in a stately dance as you pass them, the acacias raise their flattened umbrellas and thorn trees cut lacy designs. However huge their trunks, the trees along the river, like all the trees in Africa, are delicately foliated, exhibiting the monkeys and birds on their branches, letting in the sky.

The last morning, when the Land Rover exerted a certain familiar will of its own to which Bob yielded the wheel, it not unnaturally turned its head north, away from the river, and up a worsening road to a rocky pinnacle which we got out and climbed. The top commanded a tremendous panorama of that gateway to the north and an equally vast view back all the way to Mount Kenya nearly a hundred miles away. Seen through our glasses it was sharp-rocked and bitten with glaciers, a cruel-looking peak with longer shoulders than Kilimanjaro — less beautiful and far more fearful.

Nearer to, the strange old mountains ahead of us looked stranger still. One, flat as a table on top and rather like Half Dome in Yosemite, had smooth two-thousand-foot cliffs curving over in a giant fall of rock. Next to it was a massive mountain which Bob had visited — covered with forest and wild streams and gorges in whose caves the Samburu men have their meat-eating hideouts, leaving bones strewn about on the earth floor and paintings on the walls, exactly like prehistoric men — and what, after all, *is* prehistory here except everything over a hundred years ago? Far below us on the floor of the plain, two herds of goats flowed over the bare ground among the thorn trees, ahead of their Samburu herdsmen. They were coming from the north.

All the vegetation, as far as we could see, looked dead. Down along the river it was green, the thorn trees were in bloom and dangled soft little caterpillars of flower but away from the river they were preserving their moisture and showed only their thorns; looking across, or through them, they were as bristling white as if there had been a heavy frost. Scattered here and there between them was a tree like a small and terribly twisted crab apple, its bark of the most astonishing colors: many shades of reds and greens and a pure robin's-egg blue. Yet however dry and sticklike every tree and bush appeared, it still contained a reservoir of moisture: if you broke one of the rare green beads of bud off a thorn, it was at once replaced by a fat drop of sticky milk. This kind of secretion is the only fluid needed by the gerenuk — an attenuated, long-necked gazelle who thrives in the desert and never goes near water. Perfectly attuned to his surroundings, he has hooves like the feet and slippers of ballet dancers, which allow him to stand for long periods of time on his delicate hind legs while he plucks delicacies off the tops of bushes and small trees. He is an embodiment of the desert — its pale colors, twigs and sun dapple, the darker branches of its trees refined into his gently ridged and curving horns. You feel that if there were a sudden gust of wind, or you blinked your eyes, he might no longer be there. We had photographed and gazed at many of them; that morning, incredibly, we saw a pure white buck — a creature out of a myth.

The land we explored the morning before, though nearer the river, had appeared to be totally without life, and among ourselves there was either silence or wry speculation as to why Bob had come this way. When we had left our bandas after morning tea, the baboons were still asleep in the trees, mostly in twos and with an arm around one another. "The *animals* know better than to get up as early as we do," said Nat in a gently reproving tone; Bob made no attempt to defend himself, just drove quietly about, turning the wheel to avoid a termite mound or take a new track, the Land Rover creaking along.

And suddenly, quite close, there were six elephants. The biggest, a cow, with the udders up between her front legs very full, got wind of us: she tossed her trunk in the air, waved her massive head this way and that as though shaking something intolerable away and trumpeted; then, tucking her trunk between her legs and spreading out her ears, she charged right for us. Bob swung the wheel hard over and stepped on the gas. "She could have been just making a show to warn us off," he said a little breathlessly when we were at a safe distance, "the trouble is you don't *know*. . . ."

A little farther on we found a herd of thirty-five or more,

slowly moving in a great phalanx toward the river — all abreast. It is very hard to count elephants: they overlap like layers of rock, like massed boulders. Ears fanning in and out, they slowly grew in size as they came toward us, their trunks as ringed as palm boles in front, the undersides looking like great caterpillars. One baby stopped to nurse; another, its ears flattened to its skull, was like a little old shawled woman. Across the road from them, watching them too, stood a single eland — a square, solid fellow, his dewlaps hanging in carved folds. In the early light, in that spare land — all earth and rock and dust-colored, he was a sculpture from a prehistoric cave.

By noon the elephants had reached the river; on a nearby bluff we sat and watched them. Some, already finished with their baths, had recrossed the river; others were fording it, drinking or defecating as they went; a group of twelve or fifteen were still in a small cove, bathing. They covered themselves with mud, using both trunk and legs to spread it around; sprayed themselves with water; climbed out onto the bank and rubbed against tree trunks and powdered themselves all over with dust blown out of their trunks in clouds — all in the slowest, most deliberate rhythm. Many put their rear ends against the bank and rubbed them back and forth, a silly beatific smile on their faces. Once there was a panic — raising of trunks, screaming, and some lunged our way, but it must have been a quarrel among themselves for all quieted down again. Fording the river, one after another, some with trunk laid over a tusk, they splashed solemnly across the wide stream and gradually dissolved into the trees and onto the other shore. Elephants disappear as mysteriously as they arrive. They seem less to move into

sight than to materialize out of their backgrounds of forest or desert — warm earth color in the open sunshine of the latter, gray cliffs and ledges in the shade. They don't vanish rapidly as other animals do but melt into the tapestry from which they emerged, an ear or trunk or flank which was visible a moment before so woven into light and shadow that you realize too late it is no longer there. They are like the earth itself given breath and perception — feeling and feeding and moving toward its own inscrutable ends.

Our real farewell to the animals, the north country — to Eden — took place that afternoon. We headed westward along the road that follows the river and as if on cue and arranged by some super-impresario, animals, birds, even trees

and sky made special appearances, graced us with their presence and withdrew into night. The Ewaso Nyiro in the
lowering sun was a wide river of light between its trees; at
one point eight buffalo were fording it, dragging their reflections along with them, and on a sand bar sat a community
of baboons. Presently, from the occupants of another car we
learned through sign language and excited pointings that a
leopard was hiding between them and the river. As soon as
they had left Bob turned off the road at right angles to the
river, figuring that the leopard might want to get away from
it himself now and that we could head him off. He and the
leopard acted at the same instant: it crossed the road in front
of us and slipped inside a bush. We made a wide circle

around and waited and then it was two leopards who furtively and carefully crossed an open space between big bushes. The first, very golden, turned and stared for a long moment with the sun full in its eyes — a look narrower, more calculating, much wilder than a lion's. It was followed shortly by a young leopard, smaller and paler and more frightened: belly almost to the ground, not looking right or left, it hurried to catch up.

On the far bank of the river when we returned to it, a procession of beautiful vulturine guinea fowl was going down to the water to drink. With the orderliness of all the wild at water, those in the rear waited patiently and those who had finished moved aside to make way for newcomers, while in a kind of chorus line eight or ten birds daintily dipped their beaks in at a time, lifting their heads to let the water trickle down their long throats. The brilliant blue and white feathers festooning their chests shone like sapphire in the river's light; sometimes the sun lit a ruby eye or the ginger ruff at the back of a head. As far as one could see, a long, continuous line of birds poured in a blue and white stream out of the forest. Nearby a group of giraffes was drinking, too — each waiting patiently behind the one at the brink who, with front feet spread out sideways in a clumsily graceful obeisance, lowered its mouth to the river's face.

Although we had seen many dik-dik in the past weeks, it remained for this last evening to show us three, grouped like some exquisite sculpture, only a few yards away. For once we had a chance to study them at leisure: their size — about that of a whippet; their extreme delicacy of leg and hoof and ear — above all of movement; their enormous soft eyes — liquid as the eyes of rabbit and mouse, and the black comma in the corner like a black tear. The male turned his head with its sprightly two-inch horns to look at us; we saw the fuzzy little topknots between the ears on the female and on her nearly grown child. They seemed quite unperturbed and, unlike most dik dik, unconcerned about getting away. Perhaps it was the deepening dark and their getting settled for the night — like the herd of impala, thirty or more, gathered in the next circular glade right beside the road. They too stood quietly, only turning heads or ears our way — arranged as if in a Persian miniature.

When we came out again into more open country, the sun had set, all that was left to mark its going a single curve of gold cloud, like a lifted wing. Against the deepening pink in the sky, acacias and palms and, beyond them, the breast-shaped hills — drew their black outlines. High up, clear and limpid, the new moon floated on its back and Venus sparkled. Always the twilights were completely different from the dawns: even with the same degree of light I believe that if without knowing the time of day, one were set into the one or the other it would be unmistakable which it was. Where the dawns are brilliant, fresh, full of promise, the twilight is all gentle and mellow — so complete as to bring tears of fulfillment.

In this gentleness, as we rounded a curve, we came face to face with the long lifted heads of three giraffes framed in a vignette of leaves. They gazed in their usual calm, interested yet detached way, then walked unhurriedly off — the motion of their bodies transferring itself in a gentle undulation along their manes. After a few paces all three stopped and turned around, gave us another long and inquisitive look and withdrew. My heart and eyes filled, it was so much as if the characters in a play returned before the curtain — with perfect grace and innocence — to acknowledge our communion and then depart.

I have often found myself moved by this moment in the theater out of all proportion to what was actually taking place there on the stage: why should a handful of actors in their costumes and grease paint and already having discarded like an overcoat the spell of their parts, produce such a powerful effect? A very wise man of the theater with whom I once watched the scene of the players leaving at the end of *The Taming of the Shrew* suggested that unconscious memories of the race are stirred, "players" having once been looked upon as beings with unusual, almost supernatural powers. My own feeling is that it is a powerful reminder that all of us — merely by having been born into life — are cast in roles, are actors on a stage, and that the players' departure illustrates for us our longed-for resolution and release. That evening, when everything was so deepened for us by our coming departure, one creature after another had come before us virtually saying: this is as you have come to know me — in these spots, wearing these feathers, my head growing these horns — when, in fact, they are only the costumes for the part I was put here to play. In reality, I belong, like you, to the same whole; we are not so different as this getup and the things I am asked to do have made you believe.

It was nearly night. On the soft sandy road the car moved quietly and smoothly. Where I stood in the open hatch, the evening air, warmly cool, flowed gently past, enveloping me like water, wafting its spicy scent — sweeter here than any-

where else we'd been, and with a breath in it of cinnamon
or of sandalwood. We drove into the lodge grounds, got out
of the Land Rover and walked toward our bandas. No one
spoke. It was like being in a temple, in a great presence.
Two of the armed guards who protected the lodge approached and whispered something, pointing with their rifle
butts across the road: right there among the bushes stood
several elephants, barely distinguishable from the night,
moving hardly more than the bushes would do in a gentle
wind.

The dreaded last dinner before returning to civilization
brought unexpected farewells of its own. Sitting together
on the porch outside the dining room, we had just drunk to
the safari and to each other when a very odd-looking per-
sonage indeed came bustling along close to the low stone
wall at our side — fussy and self-important as a door-to-door
salesman. What insect was *that* big? A locust? Some kind
of grasshopper? At its rear end it carried aloft — absolutely
straight in the air — what looked like an aerial, reminiscent
of the wart hog's comic tail-high trot, the tassel at the end
like a punctuation mark. This tassel was very dark, very
thick and — didn't it curl *over*? The cry of "Scorpion!"
brought everyone on the porch to their feet; barefoot children were picked up and set safely on chairs; the honorary
game warden of the district, who happened to be an over-
night guest at the lodge, walked determinedly off to the
kitchen and returned with a beer mug. What was he going
to do with the scorpion, I asked him when it was safely
inside the mug, barely visible behind all the cut glass.
Pickle him, he replied. We finished our drinks and had soup.
A fresh cluster of spectators drew me away from the table

to take another look, which I wished quickly I hadn't done: all too visible now inside a screw-topped jar, a translucent, flesh-pale object like a lobster was writhing its life away in insecticide fumes. Alive and threatening, he had at least a kind of comic if macabre dignity; now he was only pitiful and repulsive.

A moment later there was the comedy of our waiters opening bottles of champagne — terrified by the explosion of corks and the fountains of insufficiently chilled wine. And over coffee came the last touching curtain call of the evening when a toad came right up to where we sat in a series of solemn hops, each hop like a question. Without a fumble Margaret caught him and carefully returned him to the darkness between us and the river. "I've always loved them," she said wistfully, standing there staring after him, her hands still out in front of her, open — as though it were the frog-prince of the fairy tale they had just let go.

We parted for the night, not trusting ourselves to say much, and started back to our banda. Out of the night, without a word, stepped a guard with his gun. All the way to our door he shone his torch for us, its little halo of light moving across the brown dusty earth — that earth which now was home. At the steps I looked up at the sky, powdered with stars. The moon had gone. "Asante," we whispered to the almost invisible figure, thanking not only him but all that we were leaving behind.

XII

OUR WAY BACK to the twentieth-century world went through
Archer's Post, that village where the survivors of a massacre
had been settled. It was an unforgettable place — the busy
shopping center for people of several tribes, a home for the
Turkana where they could be safe and given food. Being
right out in the desert it had none of the crossroads quality
of Mto Wa Mbu which seemed, by comparison, calm and
traditional as it slowly acquired a few Western benefits.
From the name, I had expected here official buildings or at
least some European influence, but we drew up beside a large
cluster of thatch-roofed beehive huts. Bob stopped the car,
said under his breath, "Let's just see who's living here," and
disappeared. In a few moments he was back, beckoning.

Against the wall of the first hut we came to sat one of the
loveliest women I have ever seen — quiet, calm-eyed, a gra-
cious figure of bronze holding in her lap and giving a breast
to an equally beautifully formed child. His curled-up legs
and rounded buttocks, his belly circled with white beads

and his head against her — all made a composition of such curves and rounds with a matte dark surface so beautiful that it was a living sculpture of a Madonna. Between us and the center of the village there was a lot of coming and going; we walked behind a young woman wearing a full-length, very tight skirt of brown hide, supply shaped and molded and decorated here and there with small circles of beads. She had a fine figure and moved seductively — as elegant as the most worldly woman going to the opera in a Paris original.

Very quickly a crowd collected around us in the open center of the settlement. Men, particularly, pressed forward to shake our hands, bow their heads and say in deep throaty voices, "*Jambo, Memsahib; Jambo, Bwana.*" Some were quite old and white-haired; several had the bearing of elder statesmen. One man came forward addressing us in English and introduced himself as the chief; he was about forty and wore a Western sport shirt and trousers and belt; he had learned English, he told us, at the Catholic Mission.

It was a very sociable occasion, made up of many Samburu, Kikuyu and Somali of all types from the almost urban chiefs to the near-naked and primitive Turkana who had been given refuge. An African melting pot, I saw, and wished I had twice as many senses with which to take in the marvelous variety of appearances, vocal utterances, ornaments — the whole feeling of the place. The atmosphere was not only friendly, it was festive — almost febrile; then I saw out in the bare dust between huts a jeep filled with heavily armed men, carrying rifles and machine-guns, pistols, rounds of ammunition. In a few minutes the little group which had gathered around the vehicle fell back and it drove off — the soldiers' faces unsmiling and set, the dust swirling up around them. What possible good was a patrol in country like this? Every road could be conscientiously covered and the desert still hide whole bands of shifta among the light-flickering thorn trees, unthinkable atrocities be carried out.

Now young boys began to collect around us and I showed them my binoculars. Out of the group of men who had gathered around Amyas — clearly fascinated by his blond-ness, his air of relaxed authority — one stepped forward to supervise this loan. He helped the boys and reproved them if they got overeager, in a subtle way made a kind of bridge between them and me. Among the boys one stood out; he was about fourteen I would think, almost my height and ex-tremely slender, with a marvelous expression in eyes which were soft and tender yet had an exciting promise in them. Between the boy and me, as between the man and me, com-munication kept flashing, meeting, being replied to, enjoyed. How? What is it we recognize in a stranger's eye? Without any common ground or previous connection of any sort, without a single exchange of words or, in this case, much of any sign language — what is it that takes place? For some-thing very definite did: we were each other's, and utterly clear to one another, there in the milling, chattering crowd under the blinding sun. I can never forget them and some-thing of me, I feel almost sure, has stayed behind with them. It was the kind of phenomenon which is as dark and spar-kling as space.

Nearby, the others were bargaining over a massive neck-lace made of bunched strands of ostrich-shell beads — thou-sands and thousands of white circlets no larger than sequins, strung onto a ropy string dark with age. The owner, a tiny old Turkana woman, sat in front of a hut, bare-breasted and draped with other necklaces as well, her little age-shrunken head and face as hard and sharp as a monkey's. She might have been a hundred years old or more; she was wrinkled as a prune with vivid, darting eyes. Two young Samburu warriors stood against the wall, watching, resting — like cranes — on one leg. Their shining copper torsos and faces were striped and circled with zinc white; their stiffened hair extended like bird beaks right out over their foreheads. Full war paint, it looked like. They didn't smile.

The sale concluded, we had started back for the car when we were approached by someone holding out a very beautiful bead belt. I tried it on and the chief himself tied the leather thongs that fastened it, saw how well it fit and gave it and my waist a laughing little pat. Everyone looked happy and I thought the sale made but the price, we thought, was very much too high. There followed a painful few minutes of bargaining and consultations during which the belt was spirited away, recalled, and its sad-faced owner returned, shaking her head at our offer; she didn't want to sell for anything less than the high figure. When we drove off, the chief's eyes were tear-filled — I thought because of the belt and couldn't bear it: I wanted to drive right back and offer the sum, but Bob explained the chief had also hoped we would stay for tea and this we couldn't do, it was already too late.

It was one of those terrible, irretrievable little events, of no deep importance in themselves, which nevertheless leave an unhealable wound. The belt didn't matter — though it was handsome and fit me and the bargaining was stupid and irrelevant — but the misunderstanding did matter, a lot.

Contretemps of that kind, particularly among strangers from different backgrounds, have a dreadful poignancy. The thanks not given, the rebuff to outgoingness, the misunderstanding, leave a burnt hole in the fabric of communication; it can never be mended and the black edges remain. Here, with people who had suffered what they had, it seemed worse still.

I looked back at the last figures returning to their little settlement battered by the desert sun; in our forty minutes together, how much had happened! Communication had flowered and failed; we had shaken hands and understood one another across apparently uncrossable gaps — caused, and shared disappointment; we had seen soldiers off on their wilderness watch. Six weeks later, at Lake Rudolf, a similar patrol was to arrive too late: shifta had already killed — a group like ourselves. What help are soldiers in the wilderness within?

We drove on through Isiolo, made the long three-thousand-foot ascent out of the plains up to the forested ridge, and there looked back to the magic mountains: where they had stood up clear and compelling two days before, they were now nearly lost in haze, just as the Serengeti had been from the rim of the crater. At Nanyuki we stopped briefly on the Equator, at the comfortable, Tudor, Silverbeck Hotel. English club chairs and brocade curtains and paneled walls made an odd contrast to the slopes of Mount Kenya, an even odder one against the memory of Archer's Post.

The last thirty-five miles to Nyeri where we were to spend the night seemed to have no end. We were tired; it grew dark; the gazelles and steinbok running from our noise on both sides of the road were like shadows on the edge of sleep that will not come. Dusty and cold, we registered at the rambling old Outspan and were led to our rooms down endless corridors like those in dreams, which we were not at all sure we could retrace; the hot water we had anticipated for hours kept turning off so that there was a scant inch in the bottom of the tub; we were the last guests in the dining room and were hurried through. Next day the Owingses were flying back home around the world so that details of packing, flight schedules and time belts began to occupy their attention as our own travel plans absorbed ours. Bob, getting a cold, had a soft little cough he kept trying to smother; he seemed virtually as alone as if we four had already left. We were back in the time-world, among arrangements and schedules, where the future robs and kills the present. It is a never-never land, that world, and as life grows increasingly complex we spend more and more time in it.

Back in Nairobi again — for the third time, now — we became even more scattered as Margaret and Nat left for Karachi and Bob went home to bed and to be cared for by Kimani. Amyas and I spent the last afternoon shopping: for some reason it seemed dreadfully important to me to buy genuine Masai necklaces — a search which took hours and became quite obsessive — and Amyas found it equally necessary to find a three-legged Masai stool. Both of us, of course, were really trying to buy the impossible — to take home what couldn't be made — by the Masai or anyone else.

Earlier we had shopped together and become irritable and impatient with one another. I shall always hear the tone of his voice when, coming out into the street from the third or fourth bazaar stuffed with rows and rows of black wooden gazelles, birds made of horn, zebra and leopard-skin cushions and bags — all presided over by a flabby and unctuous store-keeper, he said it was hard, wasn't it, being in a city again. The surprise, the depth of hurt in his tone were echoes of those I had heard years before in the voice of our then four-year-old son — returned to a New York apartment in winter from ten days in the sun when, standing looking out at the brick wall opposite, he said, "I don't like it here." The terrible words, spoken with the terrible immediacy of childhood and vibrating at the same frequencies as his father's now, came from some depth older and wider than individual being. Where had it sprung from, that cry of protest which rang in me, too? Who, exactly, had spoken?

Next morning Bob, ill and feverish, got out of his bed and drove us to the airport — to the very end, and over our objections, doing all he could for us. We didn't let him stay till we left but rather quickly said goodbye —one of those goodbyes made so wretched by the anonymous crowd, the loudspeaker's oversized and expressionless voice, the un-remitting swirl of preflight confusion. Everything I had saved up to try and convey to him vanished like water into sand. How would he ever know, now, of that deep well of gratitude for his sensitivity and skill in helping us to see Africa not through his eyes — extraordinary as they were — but through our own? For, while consistently caring for the safety and comfort of the whole group, he had helped each one of us to enjoy in our particular way, at the same time — and how unobtrusively! — sharing with us his knowl-edge and enthusiasm, his deep cultivation. I saw the broad

back and fine head move away through the crowd of strangers — all those unknown people in saris, shorts, turbans,
English tweeds, "missing so much and so much" — and was
all but overwhelmed with the sadness of leave-taking. No
matter what the time at our disposal, or the favorability of
circumstances, we are confronted at parting by that surge of
unspoken affection, of poorly communicated closeness — is
there any help for it? And then I was staring at the green,
scratched Land Rover as it swung around the curve and out
of sight beyond a bed of blowing flowers.

A few minutes off the Nairobi airstrip we were high over
the Aberdares and still climbing. I thought I saw the road
in from the Ruhuruini Gate and the glinting curve of the
Gikiruru River, where Amyas had caught the trout. . . .

Nine hours later, in the London airport, he and I kissed
goodbye: he was flying to New York, I was staying a week
with friends in England. Few changes could have been more
abrupt or complete. All week the skies hung in a close gray
tent overhead, breaking open only twice for a few hours
each time: it was like being shut in a cellar after living in
the sky. Worse still, England's green and pleasant land —
that beautiful countryside! — felt empty and deserted and
very nearly dead. Around the lawn and in the big field
beyond, the monumental old trees stood like mourners. At
different times of day well-fed, well-behaved Holstein cattle
walked gently about, grazing, and vanished again into other
pastures, — an orderly and subdued chorus on an empty
stage. Rarely, a dove murmured with muffled sweetness,
"Take two coos, Taffy, take two coos," and in the hamlet
beyond the wall of the estate, a dog barked. Little dun-
colored birds perched on fences or flapped across the dark

sky. The whole landscape was crowded with absence; a world of life was gone.

Back on Long Island and in New York I was even further impoverished and dispossessed so that when a friend asked me if, after the safari, I now felt "closer to life," I hardly knew how to reply. Thoughts dashed about like fish transferred from the ocean to a pail (do *they* feel closer to water?), for after that abundance — that ocean! — in which we had been immersed, there was scarcely enough here in which to keep afloat. What an astonishing thing to feel on returning to civilization and its millions of lives! But that is just it: we are surrounded (and daily more densely) by one expression of Life only — our own — while all those other forms leading up to us, still with us from the remote past and branching out around us, are scarcely there at all. We have all but overwhelmed them. The millions of leaves obscure the tree.

In memory's sky the animals now appeared no less real but like supernatural, almost celestial creatures; I understood why the earliest representations of angels were great land beasts with wings. Another kind of angel — presences that can be counted on, they were Life being gazelle, being wart hog, being vulture. If seeing them was not quite seeing the source itself, they were manifestations of its play and so the evidence of it: Evolution's lyrics — graceful, comic, macabre — as we are its tragic, or heroic, epic. In that constant presence, how could one *not* be swept up in it? Each day in Africa my heart had almost burst with Walt Whitman's outcry: "As to me, I know of nothing else but miracles." What had been lost was the sense of being part of the miracle, the sense of belonging. I saw that the true nature of our adventure had been religious: in the earliest sense of that word — retying.

It is strange, and terrible, how unconnected we can become, what realities we are able to lose sight of. The very familiarity of people blinds us to them, just as we no longer see clearly those who are closest to us until coming on them unprepared — in an unexpected place, even in a forgotten photograph — when suddenly and with a twist of the heart, we see how beautiful, how extraordinary they are. Watching the daily lives of so many kinds of created beings, close to us yet different, it was as if, having known of the night sky only the moon and a few planets, one found oneself for the first time under the whole incredible company of stars. The treasure it is to be alive and sentient, and the miracle of the evolution of consciousness was upon us, shining from a million million points.

Most of all, the myriad creatures were a key to what we are. Western man has done, and made, so much that we have developed a curiously distorted sense of ourselves — already clouded by our particular circumstances and their encrustations of images. We act as if we had forgotten we are creatures — another kind of animal — that "the Lord . . . made us, and not we ourselves." In our depths we have *not* forgotten: the abyss between that humble self-knowledge and man's pride, at this peak of his *hubris* and technical genius, almost tears us apart till we murder each other in self-loathing and want to blow up the earth.

We are all creatures of the earth, the animals said; *the earth is our strength and home.* And I remembered how from high up in a New York apartment building, our three-year-old daughter used to wave goodbye to me across the

street, fifteen floors below: she looked like a small bright
butterfly up there, behind the glass, and I would marvel how
far civilization had taken our feet from earth — and think
of Antaeus, that giant of strength who, when Hercules lifted
him off the ground, strangled in the air. We need the actual
soil — loam and rock, mud and sand and, metaphorically,
the whole earth of our past and of our natural being. *We
are your past,* said all that life; *we are the world out of which
you grew.*

And they were messengers of what may be. All that life-
fulness related to us but without our particular attributes,
magnified the glory of language and art, of reason and of
love, while the limitations of the monkey, the circumscrip-
tion of even so splendid a creature as the lion showed how
possibilities of being surround us like space itself. *Because
you are you* (the animals said) — *an expression of Life beyond what we are — your possibilities for order and harmony
are greater by the degree of another whole dimension: that
of your human consciousness.*

I do not find it difficult to believe that consciousness has
its own dimensions, analogous to those of space. Even in
the seventh century the Chinese sage Hui-Neng compared
the capacity of the mind to the emptiness of space, and spoke
of the "truly sky-like quality" of the natural self. As consciousness became more complex, it left the straight line
between perception and obedience-to-instinct, and moved
into the field of valuing, choosing, imagining, while at moments in our lives which stand out for their unfamiliar and
stirring nature — as though they were visitations — we sense
that there may be dimensions beyond any we already know:
freer, clearer, in more immediate harmony with some larger

reality. We recognize, then, how restricted we ordinarily are — as if man had "fallen asleep in matter and time and in himself" but need not remain so. In some blessed, mysterious way artists succeed from time to time in giving us intimations of such a state: "God's spies," they are the scouts returned to tell us of it.

There is a definition of a poet — though it could apply to all of us — as "a sea-creature living on land and longing for the air." The sea: those ancient waters of darkness of the Vedic myths, out of which the cosmos and everything in it evolved and into which — when exhausted — it will once again be absorbed until such time as it reappears. This is the breathing of the god Vishnu, the pulsating universe of twentieth-century physics. The land: where we are. The air (or sky): that free, illimitable element where the medievalist set his angels and Einstein saw timelessness and the curvature of light; element we are now invading; symbol of the infinity of possibilities arched over every moment.

The possibilities of what we might be, and become, feel as limitless. Why should the Great Imagination that worked from the long-chain molecule to the inventing and devastating mind of man content itself with what we now are? The bond of affection, says Konrad Lorentz, appeared in the animal world only comparatively recently and we came later than they. The sense of community, in us, like the inhibition of violence, is scarcely more as yet than a dream.

The "air" for which we long is invisible, the earth is at our feet. I think of our happiness on the peak of Ngurdoto — surrounded by all that empty space, the aerial mating of hawks over our heads: our foothold on earth had never seemed more precious nor the sky so full of promise. *You are both of the earth and of the sky,* they said: *the instincts you think you have lost, the qualities you don't yet know exist. You are the bridge.*

That airy platform of the East African Highland is our earth — the mothering abundance of Creation. But if, on coming away, I had lost it, I knew, now, that it *is, there.* I knew that high in the blazing light, herds gallop and graze in the open plains; lions lie deep in the lion-colored grass, leopards rest in the sun-spotted shade. I knew that baboon families cluster like fruit in the fever trees along banks of streams, barking with alarm, screaming with dismay; that touraco open hibiscus wings to carry them to the next tree, and hippos send a wash of muddy ripples up the banks of rivers as they move under their own bow waves to fresh pastures. The whole concerto is still being played. It is only that I am no longer there to hear.